AN (EXTRA)ORDINARY LIFE

From a childhood in Royton to tank warfare in North Africa and Italy

Frank Ashworth

ELSP

Published in 2020 by ELSP

Origination by Seaflower Books
www.ex-librisbooks.co.uk

Printed by CPI Antony Rowe
Chippenham, Wiltshire

CONTENTS

PREFACE

I am now 90 years of age, and feel a lucky man as I have a lovely wife, Maureen, a lovely daughter Brenda, three grandchildren and even six great grandchildren.

It has not always been a good life. Looking back on it now some people would consider it an extraordinary life in many ways, especially the young folk, for whom I am writing this as they requested.

My dear wife Maureen took my dictation and painstakingly set it down for me, which I wanted to do before my memory went. It is my hope that they may learn something of history during my lifetime.

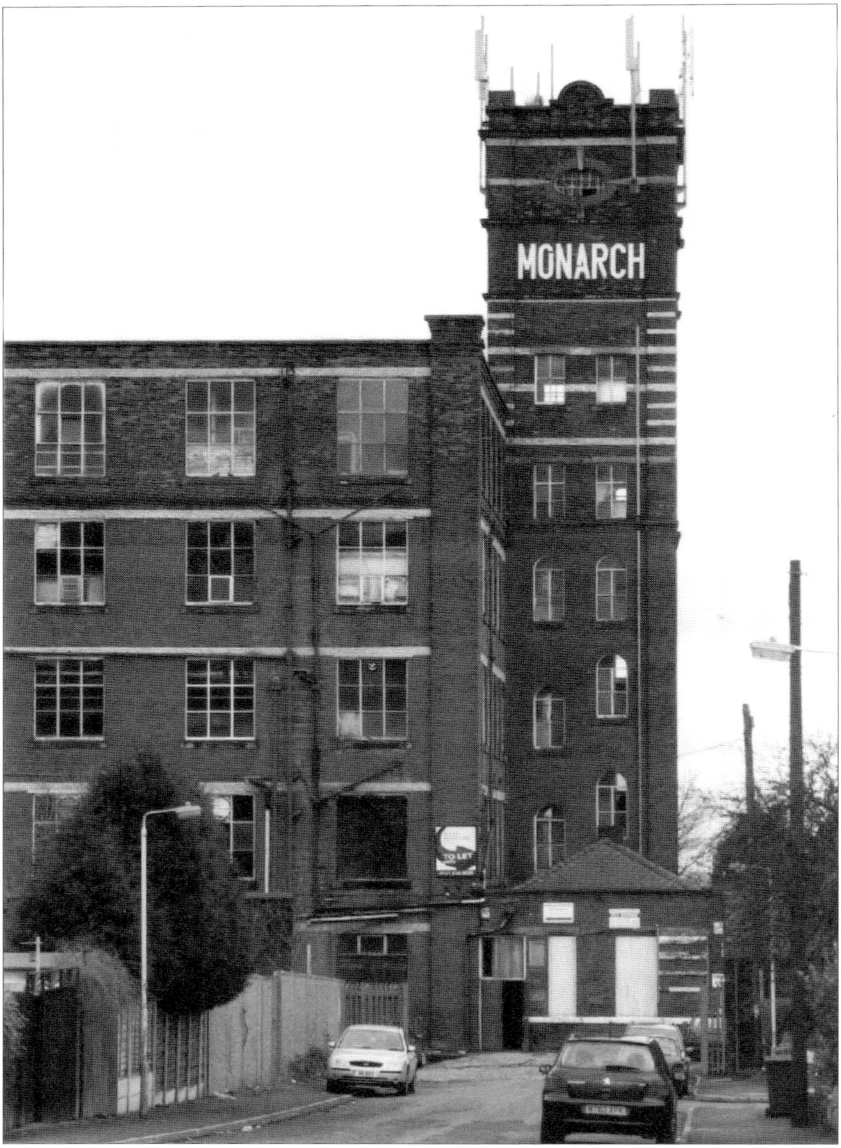

Monarch Mill, Royton; demolished 2005

CHAPTER ONE

Childhood in Royton

I was born on the 1st of April 1922, not an auspicious beginning. My mother and father were both cotton operatives, though unemployed as many were in those days, the cotton industry having practically closed down owing to not getting cotton from America or Egypt. My father Sydney Ashworth was the eldest child of Joseph Ashworth and Florence Lavinia (*née* Till) of Walsall. My mother Bessie (*née* Crosland) was the youngest child of Sam Batley Crosland and Annie (*née* Brown) and was born at The Milking Green, Lees, near Oldham. They rented a back room of a four-room terraced house in Sheppard Street in Royton, Lancashire, which was all they could afford on the dole as it was then; one of the conditions of the lease was that no children were allowed. I already had an older brother, Ernest, who had been sent to live with my maternal grandfather, Sam Crosland, and his daughter my Aunt Cissy, who also lived in a four-room terraced house at 16 Eleanor Road, Royton.

I appeared on the scene, not really welcome and, when I was only three weeks old, we were evicted.

My paternal grandmother, Florence Lavinia Ashworth, could accommodate my father but had no room for me and Mam, as her son Alfred and daughter Elsie were also living with her. So Mam and I had to go to Oldham Workhouse, and it was there I had my first birthday. Eventually my father managed to rent a room over the workshop of Mr Sladen the saddler. This was where my younger brother Harry was born, again probably not welcome, but there was no birth control in those days. My brother Ernest was still with Grandad. After a couple of years we moved to a cheaper place, a Gipsy type caravan, a little wooden affair on the green near Grandad's house.

It is here that my memories start.

I remember the caravan: it had big wooden wheels, a little platform at the front, wooden steps up to the platform, and shafts for a horse. Inside at the back was a large wooden shelf, where Mam and Dad had a straw mattress and that was their bed. Harry and I slept under the large shelf on the floor. There was a tiny cast iron stove for cooking and heating and a small paraffin lamp for lighting. Once a year with the help of friends, Dad had to lift the caravan and turn the wheels a full revolution, with the aid of a long piece of wood as a lever, so that we would not have to pay the rates. I vividly remember all the family scraping the ground on which the caravan stood to get bits of coal, this ground was known locally as "The Coalpit Hills", as years before people in extreme poverty had scraped small pits there. We had no sewage laid on, so each day Dad or Mam would carry the slops bucket to Grandad's back yard, then empty it down the outside lavatory.

It was at this time that I started school at St Anne's Infants School.

About twenty yards to the right of our caravan was Royton Harriers Hut, where my cousin Sam was a champion runner. I used to go into the hut at the end of a race when all the runners would bathe in a large square communal bath. There were no lady runners in those days, and I was very shocked when the ladies brought extra buckets of hot water from an outside boiler to the bath, when the men had nothing on. I told my Mam I thought they were very rude.

Eventually we moved to 270 Oldham Road. We had two rooms in another four-room terraced house, the back room downstairs which was our living room and the front room upstairs for our bedroom. We all slept in the one bedroom which had two beds, Dad and Mam in one bed, Ernest, Harry and I in the other bed, my older brother Ernest having come back to live with us. There were endless fights between us boys as we fought to have equal space, or someone had cold feet they were warming on someone else, or they turned the wrong way. We slept in order of seniority, Ernest and I at the top and Harry being the youngest slept at the bottom between our sweaty feet. Although we were crushed in, it did have advantages in that we kept each other warm during the cold winter nights, much better than being in a bed on your own.

My youngest brother Joe was born in this house. We children were told to go outside to play one day, and not to come back in until told to. When we did come in, there was Joseph. A large drawer from the base of the wardrobe was made into a cot for him and he slept quite happily in this.

Winters seemed much colder then as we rarely had enough coal to keep the living room fire going, but when we did have a fire we would heat two bricks in the fire during the evening, then wrap them in some old material and put them in our beds to warm them. That of course sparked more fights, as you cannot get six feet on one brick! We never had any pyjamas or nightclothes so would sleep in our underwear such as it was, then in the morning would pull all our other clothes into the bed to warm them up before getting dressed under the bed clothes and emerging fully dressed. We then only needed a quick wash under the cold tap in the living room.

A sight that always fascinated us was the beautiful fern-like patterns formed in ice on the inside of the windows by the condensation from our breath during the night, but which we were told was made by Jack Frost. I have never seen this since my childhood, probably because houses are so much warmer and better insulated now.

Our downstairs living room had a stone floor, which then was called a "flagstone floor". These floors were very cold, so we all kept our clogs on all the time. Mam made a "peg rug" to go in front of the fire. These were made from strips of any old material no matter what the colour or thickness. Then using a rug hook these strips of material were pulled through a piece of sacking (usually an old potato sack) to make a surprisingly pretty mosaic pattern rug of a good thickness.

On one wall of the living room we had a slop stone, which is a flattish sink with a cold-water tap over it, and on this stood a wooden box with sand in it. This was the scouring agent to clean the cast iron pans or anything else difficult to clean. Near the slop stone we had a wooden wringer with large rollers and a big handle to turn the rollers. On washdays we children had to turn the handle while Mam pushed the laundry through to wring out most of the water. A long rack with five slats was fastened to the ceiling by pulleys, and in winter when we could not put the washing out in the back yard to dry, it was draped over the rack, and hauled up to the ceiling to be left there until everything was dry, and ready to iron. The iron was the old flat iron on a stand, and the iron was put on the stove to heat up, and to test it for heat you spat on it to see if it sizzled, and if so it was hot enough to iron with.

Set in the chimneybreast was a huge cast iron fireplace with an oven on one side and the boiler on the other, where a heavy cast iron kettle was always on the hob full of nearly boiling water, ready in case anyone called. Above this opening was the solid mantelpiece and above that a solitary gas lamp. The stove was cleaned every week with black lead polish until it gleamed, and as we got older, this job was passed on to us boys. A square kitchen table was in the middle of the room with two chairs. At meal times we often had newspapers to cover the table in place of a tablecloth, which was kept for best, and we were told it was bad manners to read the papers while eating. We children were not allowed to sit

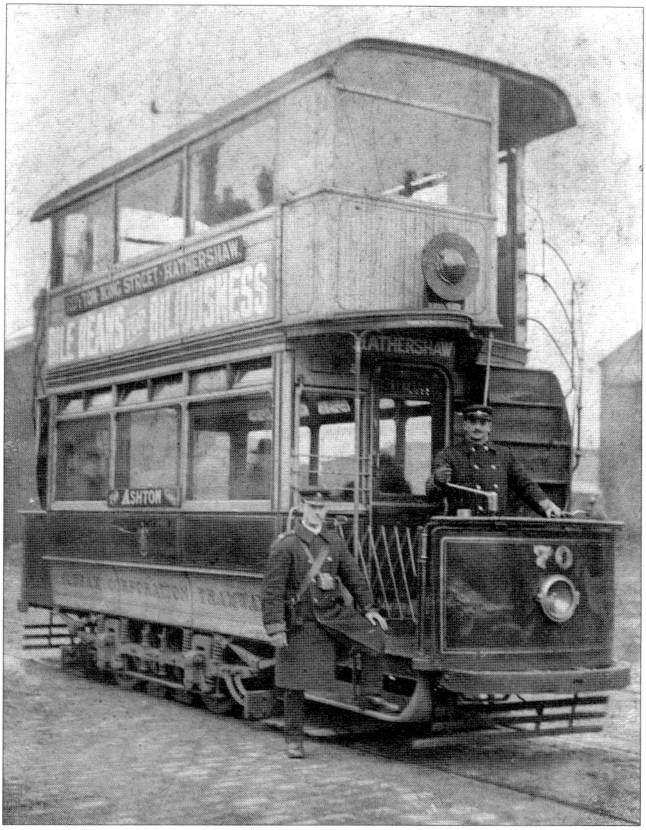

My grandfather, Sam Crosland, Driver

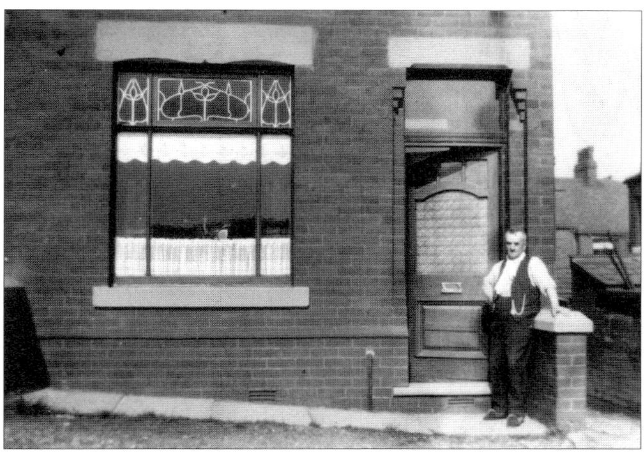

Grandfather Crosland, 16 Eleanor Road, Royton

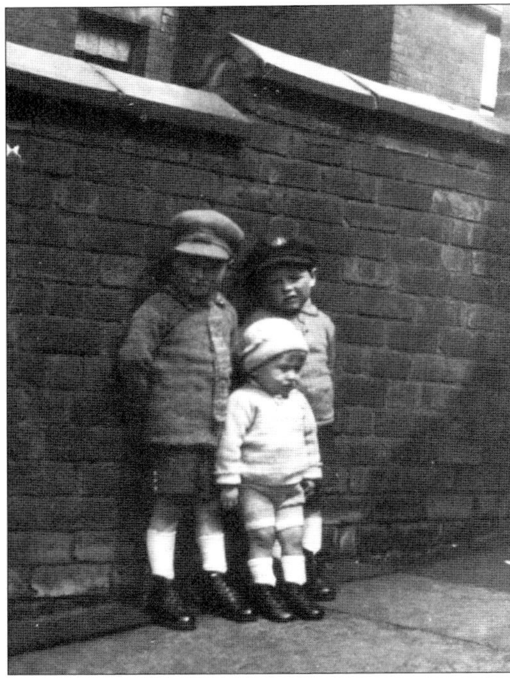

In Granddad's backyard: Ernest; Frank; Harry

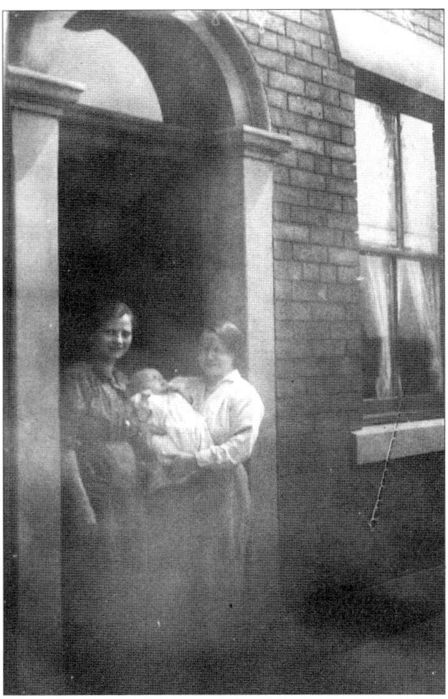

I was born in this house in Shepherd Street, Royton. My mother and myself being held a friend

down during meals. We were told that when eating children must always have a straight and open stomach, making it strong and avoiding any troubles, but as I remember we had only two chairs occupied by Mam and Dad, so perhaps that was the reason we were told this! We were also not allowed to drink during meals, as they said it would create good saliva to digest food with, but we could have as much water as we liked before or after, but not when eating. We never had any cordials or soft drinks in those days, as we could not afford to buy any, so it was always water. I do not know if it is because of these rulings by my parents, but thankfully I have never had any stomach problems.

There was an outside toilet, which we were loathe to use in winter, but I remember that there was a very large rusty sword blade in the corner, and it was not until about twenty years later that I found out it belonged to the brother of Grandmother Crosland. Seemingly he was so tall, over seven feet, that no one would employ him locally. He was forced to join the army where his uniform and everything was made to measure for him, and that was his sword. By the time I found this out, the sword had disappeared, but I would love to have been able to get it to restore.

One of the drawbacks of living in this house was that another family lived in the other two rooms, and as there was only one tap in the house, which was in our downstairs room, they had to come through our room to get water. They also had to come through to go to the outside toilet. It was very embarrassing for me as a young child when bath night came round on Saturday. We had a tin bath which was put in front of the fire, and we all had to take our turn to sit in the same water, youngest first, which was Joe, then Harry, then myself, and last came Ernest. For me it was very embarrassing when the other family came through our room while I was sitting in the bath. Then we all had to go to bed, while Mam and Dad had a bath.

My mother took in washing to help out with living expenses,

and when it was washed, dried and ironed, no mean feat in those days all done by hand, I had to deliver it back to the owners. I had to wait until it was dark so that no one would guess what I was doing, because if I had been seen and it was found out what Mam was doing, the wage she got of two shillings would be deducted by the means test from the unemployment benefit Dad got, of 16s.0d a week for a family of six.

With 270 Oldham Road being on a main road we could hear the cries of the salesmen.

The coalman for instance used to shout, "Coal, coal one and six a bag, coal". Another one, the pie and pea man would call, "Peas, Peas all hot, bring your pot and I'll give you a lot". He had on a white coat, and carried a yoke across his shoulders from which brass pans hung, and these had a paraffin fire underneath. He would carry this around and people would bring their pots to him, which he would fill for a penny.

Then there was the ragman, his call was, "Any old rags, donkey rubbing stones". The donkey rubbing stones were used to scrub the front door steps, and some ladies even cleaned the pavement. They brought the steps up beautifully white and clean looking. Any lady who did not keep their step clean was considered very slovenly.

The knife grinder with his call of "Knives and scissors to grind" would set up his wooden framed contraption with a grindstone which he would turn with a pedal by one foot, leaving his hands free to sharpen the knives and scissors.

We also had a window cleaner who did his rounds in our district, and his cry was "I'll clean your filthy windows". Just as a point of interest we used to call this window cleaner the "Longsight Fire Brigade", the reason being that to make it easier for himself he had a bicycle on which he balanced his ladder on one side, with a bucket of water on the other side. We said he was the fire brigade because we thought he would be able to put his ladder up to a building and throw his bucket of water into the flames. Eventually

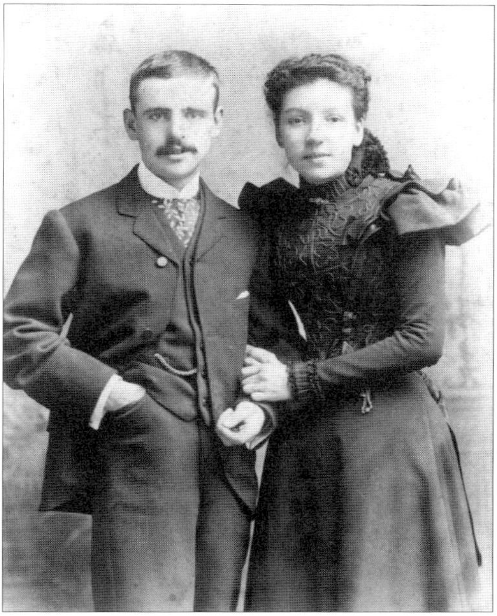

Grandfather Joseph, 1877-1922, and grandmother Florence Lavinia Ashworth, 1877-1969

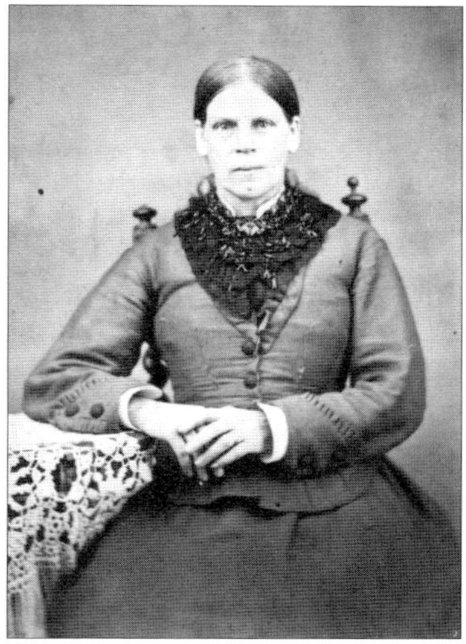

Grandmother Till (Walsall), mother of Florence Lavinia

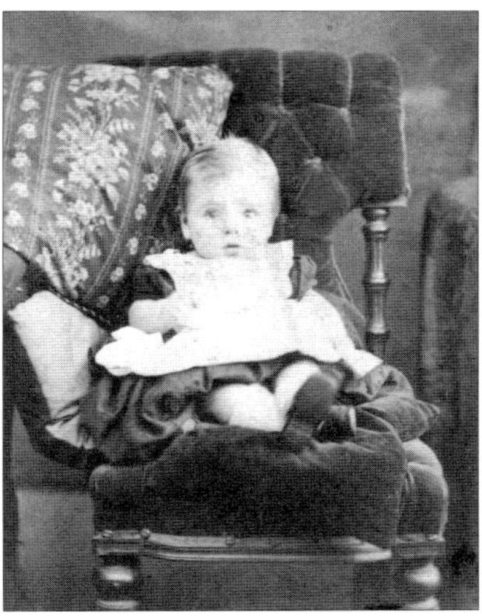

My grandfather Ashworth, aged 8 months, 1878

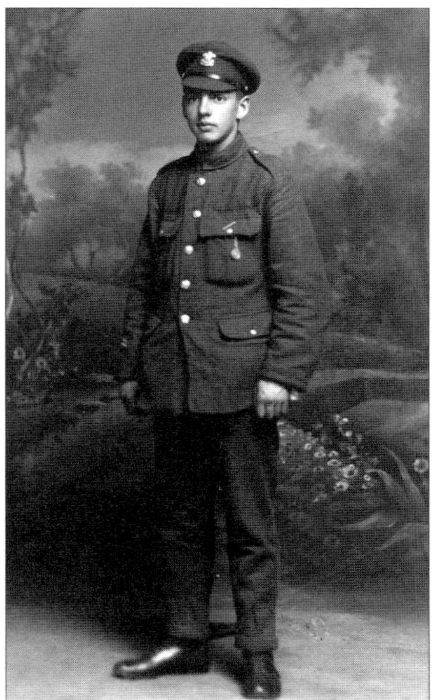

My father Sydney, 1899-1978

he improved himself and bought a donkey and cart to carry his ladders and water bucket. One day doing the top floor of a house he found he could not reach, so he backed up the donkey until the cart was under the window then put his ladders in the cart to reach the window. While he was at the top of the ladder the donkey walked away, and he came tumbling down, but luckily he was not seriously injured, although it gave us all a laugh, poor man. He had a store or stable in which he kept the donkey near the back of our house, there was a window in it, and I used to like looking through to see the donkey. One morning I was passing and looked in and to my horror saw this poor man had hanged himself in there, and the donkey was still placidly chewing. I told a neighbour, and they called the police to see to him. It was something I did not forget in a hurry and still can picture it vividly to this day.

Another incident I would never forget was another suicide I found. Not far from my junior school there was a stream and one day I found this lady who had managed to drown herself although it was not very deep. To make this even sadder, she was the mother of one of my classmates.

It seems I was fated to see another sad event during my boyhood, as about six of my mates and me were sitting on a wall by the Monarch Mill when we saw a man walk along the roof and throw himself off the other side. We found out that he actually fell onto the roof of the engine house, which broke his fall and he did not die. However, when he recovered he was taken to court, as he had been embezzling money, and this was the reason he tried to commit suicide.

One thing that was a must for every boy then was a handcart. I remember begging a wooden box from the Co-Op Grocery Store, an axle and two wheels from an old pram from someone, and then put two handles on it. This earned me quite a lot of money, mainly by going to the gasworks about two miles away for coke, which the neighbours would ask me to fetch, at that time coke being the

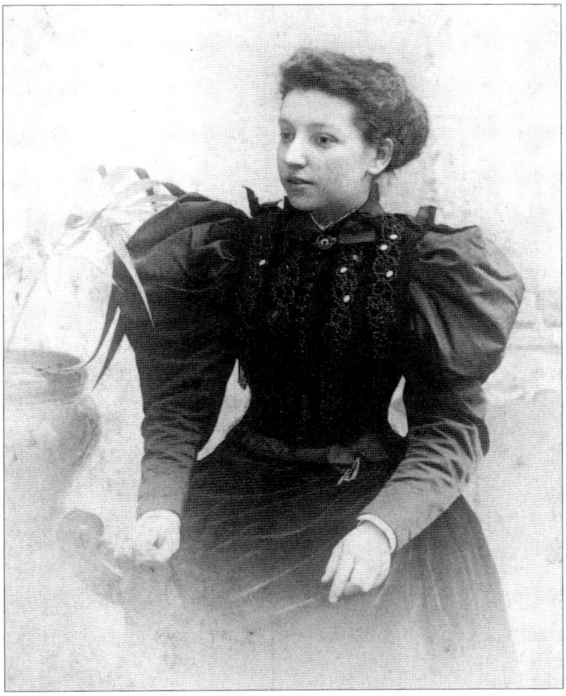

Grandmother Ashworth, aged 18 years

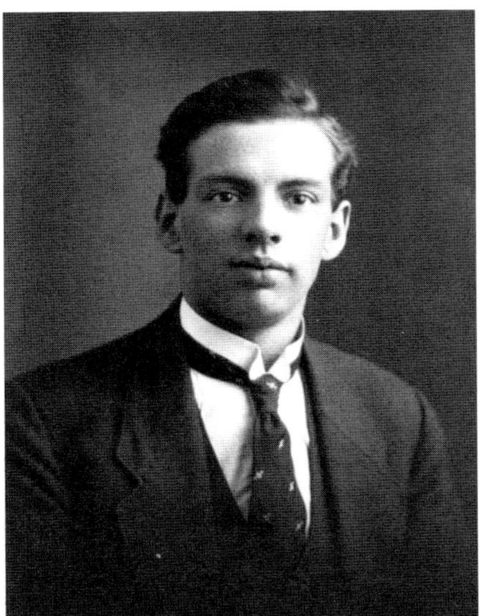

My father Sydney, aged 19 years

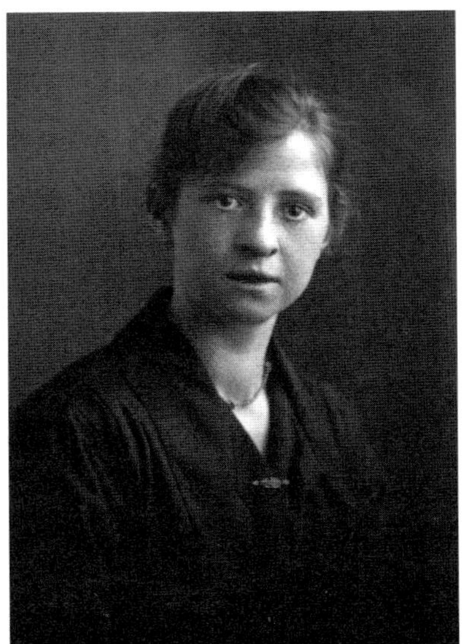

My mother Bessie, aged 19 years

cheapest fuel available. I also ran errands getting heavy items from the grocers for people.

In those days, we could not afford a ball to play with, so we would go to the pork butcher and ask him for a pig's bladder. He was the old type butcher who would go to market and buy a pig, which would then be taken to the back of the shop where he would slaughter it himself. He would give us the bladder, which we would blow up and tie a knot on, and then we had a very good ball. Well, to us it seemed good anyway.

I recall that the house at 270 Oldham Road was a rather miserable place. It was rather dark, as we had gaslight, which was probably the equivalent of a forty-watt bulb these days. It had a mantle that was very fragile, and if you touched it, it would break. Then you had to run out and buy another one, which would cost a penny, from old Jane's shop, about 30 yards away across the road. Old Jane as we called her always dressed in black clothes that came to the floor and she wore clogs, she would come through from her living room when the little bell on a spring rang when you opened her door. Her shop was her front room and she stocked bread, cigarettes, matches, reels of cotton and wools for darning socks, the gas mantles and all sorts of everyday needs. She would put things on tick for you, and had a number of slates on which she chalked what was owed, this debt would be cleared monthly but, as was the custom, you cleared your debt at the end of the year before New Year's Day, or you would have bad luck. This tale was probably told, so that you would at least clear your debt sometime!

My Mam's brother Uncle Fred had taken to the road and was a tramp. He called round to see her maybe about once a year, and I remember my Mam scraping up 2p to send me to Old Jane's to buy a packet of five Club cigarettes for him, and then she would give him a meal before he disappeared again for another year.

Sometimes Grandad would take my brother Ernest and myself to the market in Oldham, called the "Tommy Field Market", and of course we had to walk there. He always took us to the "Duck a Muffin" shop where he would buy us a halfpenny one, which consisted of a muffin cut like a purse, filled with meat and gravy, and the gravy ran down your chin. Aunt Cissie would also take us sometimes, and we would go directly to the market where she would buy us a halfpenny black pudding on a piece of paper with mustard on. It was worth the long walk to get there for these mouth-watering treats, and as the old song puts it "Oh boy, What Joy, We had in barefoot days".

* * *

CHAPTER TWO

Work, play, choirboy

I went to work for the first time when I was seven. The money was not for me to keep but to give to Mam to help with the upkeep of the family. One job was for Mr. Sladen the Saddler, he was getting on in years and found he was unable to go down to the cellar to get his coal, so he employed me to get up one bucket of coal a day for him, two on a Saturday to last him over Sunday as well, and for that he paid me one penny a day, so I earned 7 pence a week.

The other job I got was helping the butcher. I became delivery boy and took out his orders in the morning before going to school, and also helped to clean his shop. He also taught me how to skin rabbits and clean them, which was a talent I was to find very useful later in my life. He was good to me in other ways, as Mam could only afford three pence for the weekly meat ration for the six of us, and he would make sure I had more than three pennyworths to take home.

My mother was a proud little lady, and vowed that we would never go to school barefoot as many of them did in my school, even in the snows of winter. One day Ernest and I decided to take a short cut to school, although in actual fact it was probably longer but much more interesting. It was across the fields at the back of the cotton mills. A stream ran through one of the fields and we would dare one another to jump across in the wider parts. On one of these occasions, I had dared Ernest to jump across and in doing so his clog fell off and sailed merrily down the stream out of

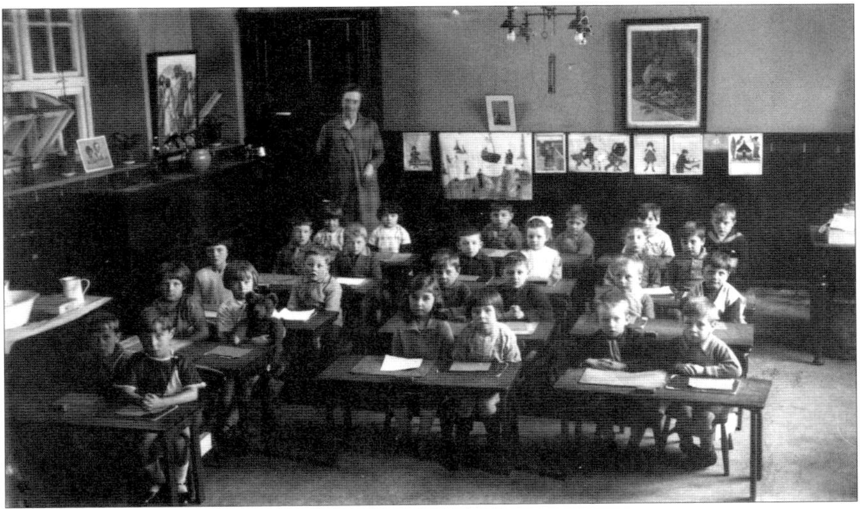

I am at the third table on left behind the teddy bear with Marjorie

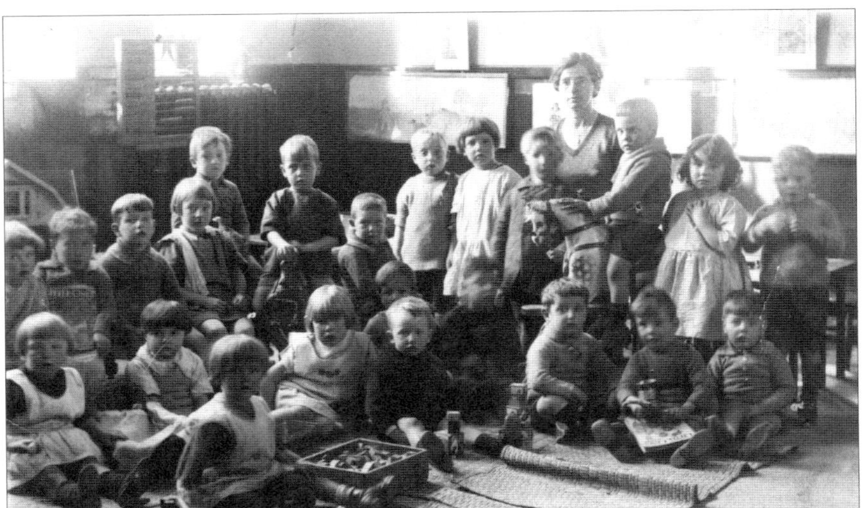

Three year-old class. I am standing at far right

sight. He was kept off school for three months while Mam saved up enough to buy new ones, which cost 1s.9d.

A dark period of my life that I remember is that my father would get drunk sometimes, maybe to alleviate the shame of unemployment, I don't know, but he would get the means test money and spend it all on drink. Then when he came home he sometimes had terrible arguments with my mother, and on occasions I have known him to hit her.

One terrible night I was in bed when I heard him come home, and there were loud shouts and screams from my mother. I got out of bed and although only wearing my shirt, as none of us had any nightclothes, I went down stairs and into the living room. There was my father with my mother pinned against the wall and he was beating her. Her face was swollen and blood was coming out of her mouth. I ran to the fireplace and grabbed the poker and hit my father. He turned round and kicked me, it was very painful as he was wearing large wooden clogs at the time, but this action quietened him and the trouble was over for that night.

An amusing thing happened when Farmer Duxbury asked Dad if he would kill a pig for him, and for payment he would get a share of the pig. Dad killed the pig, having learnt how to do this from Grandfather Ashworth who had been a butcher. Anyway the pig was shared out, but someone who must have been jealous because he did not get any, informed the police, as it was illegal to kill a pig that way. The police searched the house three times, but found nothing; the last time was when we had just finished the last piece! Forever after that my mother would call that policeman "Old Porky"!

My first love affair was when I was seven. We sat at the same table in the classroom at school, her name was Marjorie Turner, she wore lovely clothes, her hair was always clean and shining, and in it she wore coloured ribbons. I thought I would impress her, and gave her my halfpenny and my most treasured possession, my dead mouse, but to no avail. She did not want to know me. About thirty-six years later, a couple bought the hardware shop which backed onto my house, two months later the lady died, and it was only on her death I found out she was Marjorie. I wondered if she had recognised me and ever thought about my rejected dead mouse.

We always seemed to have work to do, but at times I would visit my Grandfather Crosland, with my brother Ernest. He would regale us with wonderful stories, one of his favourites being how in his youth a band of robbers had attacked him, and how he had fought them off. He had an old wooden box under his bed, which he would pull out and say that this was his treasure chest. He would tell us wonderful stories about the things inside, which were really old pieces of rubbish, but they took on a magical appearance with his words. These stories appealed to my sense of adventure though, and we would go home sword fighting with bits of wood. We found out later of course that these were all fantasy, but he took the place of radio and television for us, which was non-existent in those days, to us anyway.

Grandad also had a little leather bag in which he had about fifteen sovereigns, he would let us hold them and count them, which to us was like being in the Bank of England, as we never really had anything more than a penny for ourselves, and even that was a rarity.

Whenever we went to his house, he always asked if we had cleaned our teeth, and would make us use his method to clean them. We had to wet our forefinger in our mouth, wipe the finger at the back of the chimney, put salt on it, and then clean our teeth by rubbing with the finger. It could not have done me any harm, as even at my age now, I still have most of my teeth.

Grandad Crosland, the old reprobate, would also tell Ernest and me to fight, and the winner would get a halfpenny. Grandad would start the fight; we would use our fists or knock one another to the floor with Grandad shouting encouragement until the fight became too vicious, then he would stop it, declaring Ernest the winner and presenting him with the halfpenny. Then he would take me aside and give me a halfpenny as well, saying that Ernest won because he was the biggest but I was the best fighter. Talk about the judgement of Solomon! Another one of his tricks was to take us for a little walk. These little walks were often between twelve and fifteen miles, over to Greenfield, where he would buy us a glass of milk, then walk us back, calling at Hartshead Pike, over Oldham Edge and back to Royton. He would unbeknown to us have hidden a penny or two in different places, and then while we were walking would suddenly bend down and say, "Oh look what I have found, a penny". That would make us boys all start digging around to see if we could find any, and of course we never did.

It was at about this time that I became a choirboy at St. Anne's Church mainly because of pressure from my mother, Aunt Cissy and my Godmother Ada Taylor. Also what swayed me was the promise of an outing each year to Southport, and the uniform, which I rather liked. We had choir practice every Friday night, and we had to attend all the services, usually two on a Sunday, and on occasions three. But one thing I have never forgotten was the disappointment, and what I considered the injustice, of how members of the choir were chosen for attendance at some weddings.

When there were society weddings, and the choir was requested to attend, it was usual to give a shilling to each choirboy, which to me was a vast sum of money. However, when the practice for these weddings came around, the choirmaster would select the boys to attend. He would point to myself and any other boy who had clogs on instead of shoes and would say that we would not be required, as we would make too much noise. So those boys who could not afford shoes did not get the chance to earn a shilling either. My faith in Christianity was forever to be in doubt after this.

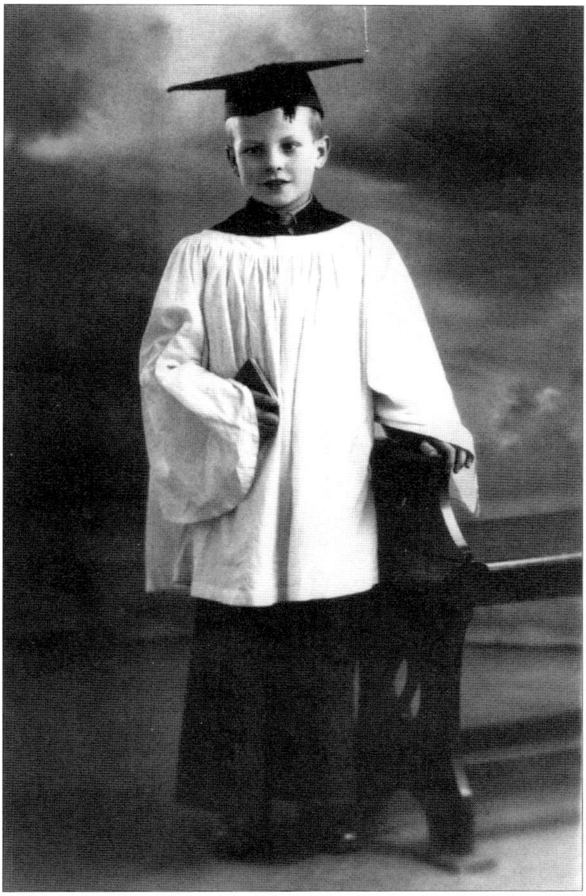

As a choirboy

At that time I was attending St. Paul's Junior School it was a very old school, a three-storey block without any playgrounds. We had to play out in the street, which was made of rounded cobblestones, so running around on them in clogs was pretty dangerous to young anklebones. I was at this school for three years, and then went on to St. Anne's Senior School.

During this time I acquired another job, in addition to the butcher and coal shifting jobs. I became a newspaper delivery boy, for the morning and evening papers. This involved getting up at about 5 a.m. to run about three quarters of a mile to the newspaper shop collect my papers and deliver them, then on to the butchers shop to take orders for him, luckily only two or three at the most in the mornings. Then go in to fetch the coal up for Mr. Sladen.

After this I would hurry home to have whatever breakfast there might or might not be, then hurry off to school. If there was no food available at home, then my brothers and I would start off ten minutes early, so that we could call in at the Methodist Chapel in Market Street, where the Salvation Army would give each child a thick slice of bread with jam on, and a mug of tea. This was quickly devoured before rushing to school.

Periodically each class of both the junior and senior schools would have to go to the Dentist. We would walk down the street in a crocodile, two by two, to the dental surgery, which was over the Post Office in Royton. On arrival we would walk up the stairs and into the surgery, then all stand round the wall facing the dentist's chair. We would then be called in alphabetical order to sit in the chair for examination and any treatment that was needed, in full view of the rest of the class. My name being Ashworth I was always the first, and of course had to put a brave face on and pretend that there was no pain, as I did not want to look a fool in front of my classmates. In those days it was rare to have a filling but if one was needed, there was no anaesthetic and it was very painful. After treatment the patient left the chair and went into the attached bathroom. In there was a chipped enamel bath with three enamel mugs, all dirty with the blood of previous victims, and you were expected to fill one of these mugs with water and swill out your mouth. Such was hygiene in those days. You would then return to the surgery and stand around watching while all the other pupils had their turn, before being marched back to school. Maybe they had a premonition that we would have to be tough in our future lives.

Another well-known visitor to the school was a nurse, she was known to everyone as "The Nit Nurse". Every class, boys and girls, would line up outside the room she was in and one by one file in to have their head inspected, then a report would be sent to the parents. In order to make sure that their children did not have lice, most parents would inspect their children's heads once a week. Mostly on a Friday night my Mam would place a page of newspaper on the table then each of us in turn would bend over the newspaper while she combed our heads with a fine tooth comb. If any nits fell out, crushing them between the thumbnails would kill them. There were many screams during this process if there were any tangles in the hair.

One way of ensuring cleanliness in the home was by decorating. Dad would go out at night with a bucket and steal half a bucket of lime from the nearest building site; he was not the only one to do this as everyone did it in those days. On returning he would fill the bucket with water and stir it up, then using a large brush would cover the ceiling and walls with the mixture. This would kill anything living in the walls. After that a packet of whitewash would be stirred into the remainder of the lime solution then the whole room would be coated in this mixture. We were then content that the room was clean for a while. This was usually done near to New Year to start the year off well. As children we looked forward to New Year as we would rush from shop to shop on New Year's Day wishing the shopkeeper "A Happy New Year" and they would then give us a little present. The greengrocer would give an apple, the baker a small cake, and the sweetshop owner would make a little cone out of a square of paper and put a couple of sweets in it for us. However we had to make sure we got round by 12 noon, as this was finishing time for treats, and then we would run home with our pockets full of goodies, and it was all over until the next year.

Another thing I remember from those days was 'The Doctor's Man'. Poor people could not afford to pay the fee for the doctor, so he employed what we called the Doctor's Man. Every Friday evening this man would visit his 'clients' houses to collect one penny from each family. These pennies would accumulate and would help towards the doctor's bill when it was necessary. A penny seems so little these days, but even that was sometimes impossible to find then. On occasions my mother would say, "When the doctor's man comes, tell him I'm out". Then she would hide upstairs until he had gone, but another week the shortage would have to be made up, which was hard.

I remember that when I was about eight years old, I visited Grandads' house, and Aunt Cissy was there, but Grandad was at work driving his tramcar from Oldham through Royton to Rochdale, and then returning on the same route, this being repeated throughout the day. Aunt Cissy asked me if I would run and meet Grandad when he reached Royton Town Hall, to take him his pack of sandwiches and his billycan of tea. I enjoyed doing this, as I got a free tram ride for two stops to Shaw Road. On this particular day I met him at Royton Town Hall and climbed up into the tramcar, it was the old type with no cover for the driver at the front or back and no roof for the upstairs passengers. I handed him his food and drink, then Grandad picked me up and put me on the knee of a gentleman sitting on the first seat, saying to me that this was a friend of his. I was terrified of him, he was dressed all in black with a tall black hat, and I had no idea why I was so frightened, but was more than pleased that day to get off at Shaw Road and run home. It was a few days later when Grandad told me that his friend was the hangman at that time, and he was on his way to Manchester Prison to hang someone.

As with most children then, my thoughts were on food a lot, and I can remember that my mother used to bake bread every week, the delicious smell is something I recall with fond memory.

She would knead the dough mixture in a large earthenware bowl, then it would be placed near the fire with a cloth over it, and this was then checked regularly to see if it had risen enough.

She would then cut the dough into loaf-sized lumps to be put in the bread tins, and again left to rise even more, before being put in the oven to bake, giving off the lovely aroma. If a little dough was left over she would make it into muffins, half cook them, then cut them open and put in a little cheese before finishing the baking. These were absolutely mouth watering, and eagerly waited for.

Other dishes I remember, perhaps never heard of these days, were tripe and onions, sheep's head broth, cow's tongue, boiled onions, and whenever possible, large bones from the butcher were cracked open and the marrow scraped out to be put into stews and hotpots etc. With added lentils and barley these would make very nourishing and filling meals, very cheaply. Puddings were usually made with suet, such as steak pudding, apple pudding, spotted dick etc. they would be wrapped in a pudding cloth which was usually a square of old sheeting kept especially for this purpose, and boiled for about three hours. Always on Mondays Mam would make what she called "Resurrection". This was any left over foods such as potatoes, vegetables, bread, meat, and rice, put in a frying pan and fried with a little fat until it was crispy, we all loved it and nothing went to waste.

One of Mam's friends, a Mrs. Lancashire, would sometimes say she had some surplus food, I now think that she did this deliberately, and would ask that I be sent to pick it up at lunch time, usually it was some potato hash or rice pudding. This helped Mam out a lot, but it was very embarrassing for me, as her son was in my class at school, and when I went to their house he very often opened the door so that I had to ask him for the leftovers. Mrs. Lancashire was very well meaning, but I suppose she did not give a thought to a young boy like me being embarrassed having to ask a classmate for his leftovers.

Once every year the school would hold a sports day, always at the Royton cricket ground. It would be marked out for all the different events, some of which I took part in. I never had the speed for the short races held on sports day, but found later in life that I had the stamina for long distances. Another day held at school was Maypole dancing day. There would be about six maypoles, which are large poles about 12 feet high, with ribbons of different colour attached to the top of them, each school having their own colour ribbons. Ours were blue and yellow, and the girls held the yellow ones, the boys the blue ones. The local Brass Band would strike a chord whereupon the boys would bow and the girls would curtsey, then the band would play the maypole tune,

"Come lasses and lads take leave of your Dads,
And away to the Maypole hie,
For every fair has a sweetheart there,
And the fiddlers standing by ..."

The boys and girls would dance around and around weaving patterns with the ribbons, so that they tightly wound round the pole to the bottom, then the judges would give points. After this the band would strike up again, and dancing round the other way would then unwind the ribbons, then again the judges gave points. It must have looked a grand sight with all the girls in their best dresses and with ribbons in their hair, the boys in their best shorts and well-polished clogs.

It seemed then that I was always stumbling on events that I should not have seen. One day when playing soldiers with a friend, I was crawling through the grass trying to keep out of sight of the "enemy", near St. Anne's tennis courts and the pavilion. We realised that this would be a good place to hide so we crawled underneath it. On the courts playing tennis with her boyfriend was my Sunday school teacher, and when they had finished playing they came into the pavilion. We then realised that the floorboards had gaps in them and we could see right into the room above. To our astonishment we saw them start to kiss and then what happened was not for our eyes, so we crawled out and ran away.

Another time some of us climbed up and were looking over the parapet of the Monarch Mill lodge. This is a pool of water used by the mill, and there we saw three young couples swimming in the nude. Our eyes were more than opened; until one of the men saw us then we turned and ran for our lives.

When I was about ten years-old, I was at home on a normal dismal day when I heard a commotion in the street, and then someone banged on the door shouting for us to come outside. We all ran out and saw everyone looking up at the sky. It was a cloudy day but pushing through the clouds was the airship R 101, it looked huge and was quite low. We all ran after it in the direction it was going, but it soon vanished in the clouds again. We had seen a couple of little biplanes before but nothing like the airship, it was quite something to remember.

During my childhood and schooldays times were very hard for everyone. Most adults were unemployed, I would say at least 70% of them, or maybe even more of the working population of the North of England. Most of these were on the means test, which was so humiliating that suicides were commonplace. Officials for the means test were by law able to enter the dwelling of anyone receiving benefit, to value any goods in that dwelling and to give orders for such items to be sold. The value of the item sold would then be deducted from the next weeks benefit. If a person on the means test were offered a job they had to accept it no matter what it was, as refusal would mean the stoppage of even the meagre amount of the benefit. So life was very hard especially for parents with children. Trying to keep children fed and clothed was almost impossible, as at that time there were no jumble sales or car boot sales, there being nothing to sell or give away.

I only remember one Christmas during my childhood when I had a present of a toy. All the other things I played with I made myself. I did occasionally receive a pair of socks, a new cap, or much later on a new pair of boots, but it was very hurtful going back to school after the Christmas holidays and the teacher would ask us to write an essay about all the things we have received and what we had done for the holidays. Most of us had to think of what we would like to have had and pretend that we had received them, so we all wrote about our wishful thinking.

We did enjoy ourselves in many ways, and what we lacked in material things we gained in other ways. We could play in the streets without worrying about traffic and being choked with the fumes. We could play or hike on the moors and be perfectly safe, as we do not remember there being anyone around at that time to be frightened of.

We had very little knowledge of hygiene and we would drink from the streams and pick fruit to eat straight from the bushes without washing them, but we never seemed to have any ill effects from this.

We considered it natural to challenge one another to ride to the coast on our bicycles to prove our fitness. We would talk about who had scored goals or a try at rugby, or we would run cross country races of a mile or three miles to prove who was the best. Now youngsters only seem to talk about what kind of shirt they have, or which designer trainers they have, or what game they have played on their computers, a totally different life.

Once I stole some rhubarb and was seen and caught by a policeman. He grabbed me by the collar and gave me a mighty whack behind the ears, then still holding my collar took me home, told my mother what I had done, and then I got another whack from her. I never stole rhubarb again!

My senior school Headmaster, Mr. Hobson, an ex-Naval Commander, was extremely strict and keen on cleanliness. At any time he would demand to inspect our hands or footwear, and if he found these were dirty, one would get a whack from his cane on the spot, so you were only ever caught out once, and then forever would make sure you were clean. What great training for your future life!

I was about ten years of age, when my friends and I joined The Band of Hope, promising never to drink alcohol. For this promise we all got a pencil and a little notebook each, which of course is why we joined. Then each week during the winter, we played games in the Methodist Chapel.

It was at about this time that I learned to swim. Not in a swimming pool, but in the only place available for us at that time, the local canal. On a warm day many of the local boys would wander down to the canal, strip off and jump in to have a swim. We younger ones would then undress and copy the older boys, and after a number of months would eventually master the art of swimming. It was a terrible place for boys to swim, because of all the rubbish and dead cats and dogs, and oil etc. in the water. It would not be allowed now, and I do not think any boys would even attempt it now. However, I do wonder if doing this, and not washing anything we had to eat like fruit etc. actually boosted our immune systems and inoculated us against a lot of viruses.

My Godmother, Ada Taylor, bought me a new cap for my birthday once. It had a lovely gold coloured lining and I was very proud of it. It was brand new, which was a very rare thing for me to have! One day I went with some of my friends to collect blackberries, and having nothing to put them in, I decided that my cap was the ideal thing. On the way home a slow moving truck passed us, and as boys did in those days, we ran after it and jumped up to hang on the back. I still had my cap in one hand so could only hang on with the other hand, and as the truck went over a bump in the road I fell off, of course landing with my cap full of berries underneath me. You can imagine the mess, and I remember very well the clip round the ears I got when I eventually plucked up courage to go home.

In many ways I am pleased that my childhood was spent in days when there was respect and good manners, and everyone helped out in bad times.

In those days a funeral would go down the middle of the road, everyone would stand and face the procession, men would take their hats off and bow, and the ladies would give a little curtsy. All other traffic came to a stand still, and even the poorer families who had to carry their own coffins would have priority.

At Whitsuntide children would have new clothes, either hand made for them or bought new, even if their parents could ill afford it. The custom was that the children would wear these new clothes to show to relatives and friends, who would then help by giving them a penny or a threepenny piece if they were lucky. All this would go to help to pay for the clothes, and of course on Whit Sunday everyone would dress in their finery, and walk behind the brass band, even the dignitaries of the Parish. The procession would go first to the Workhouse, then the hospital, and hymns would be sung. It would then proceed down the main Oldham road to the centre of Royton to meet all the other Parishes. Then with massed brass bands and thousands of the citizens of Royton would sing and play hymns, before returning to our own St Anne's Church to finish.

One thing we tend to forget is that we all spoke with a very broad Lancashire accent. Thee, thou, thine, nobut = only, Ou = he or she, yonder = there, brough or brew = hill, nowt = nothing, gassing = talking, petty = lavatory, clemin = hungry, grand = nice, and many, many more. This was Lancashire dialect, but one could tell by the way it was spoken as to where within five miles a person came from. Rochdale and Oldham are only about four miles apart but there was no mistaking the difference in their speech.

Almost opposite St. Anne's School was Mrs. Royce's Lodging House; it was opposite the "Coach and Horses" pub. I forget the exact reason why, but on one occasion I had to visit this lodging house. It was early one morning when I walked into the one large room that was the ground floor. Around this room were about two dozen single beds, and in the middle was a large pot bellied stove. An old man sat in each bed, and at the stove was old Mrs. Royce wearing only her nightdress; her bare feet were the same colour as the earth floor. She was toasting thick slices of bread at the stove, and after putting on margarine; she delivered one toast to each old man. This was their breakfast. I think they all lived there because they could not afford anything else. The Old Age Pension in those days was ten shillings a week, and that was the only treatment available for that money.

For my regular attendance at Sunday school, I was awarded the book *Swiss Family Robinson*, and the following year I got *Robinson Crusoe*. These books started my interest in adventure, and I went on to read such books as *Scot of the Antarctic*, *The Charge of the Light Brigade* and *Livingston*. Many other such books of men of valour I read, and I wondered then if I would ever have the guts to do similar deeds. I know now in my old age, that I can stand and be counted for having done my duty, and to have served with many men of the highest calibre in my squadron.

I then became a dinner boy, which involved coming out of school at midday, running to the home of a cotton mill worker where his wife would have his dinner ready in a bowl with a saucer on top with a pudding, all tied up with a red kerchief knotted on top for me to carry it to the mill without spilling any.

I had to wait while he ate his dinner then run back with the empty basin. After that I had to run home to get my own lunch and hurry back to school. After leaving school at four o'clock I would run to Royton Station and collect two fairly big bundles of newspapers from the train, then carry these back to the newsagents which was about a mile and a half away. I would then do my delivery of the evening papers before going home for tea.

In the course of time it was, thankfully for me, that poor old Mr. Sladen died, and I was relieved of my job shifting coal.

Daddy Duxbury the farmer often asked me to collect the eggs with him, including the duck eggs, which were usually found around the duck pond. Some of the eggs were soft skinned and when these were found he would make me burst them in my mouth and swallow them, this stood me in good stead during the war. At first I was squeamish about this, but soon got used to it, and I realise now that he was trying to make up for any lack of nourishment I had because of our financial position.

*

It was during this period that I joined the boy scouts, which I thoroughly enjoyed, it appealing to the adventurous side of me.

We would occasionally go to camp, some times at Tandle Hills that was only about two miles away, or further afield to Cheshire or the Yorkshire Moors, which I loved.

In those days to go to camp did not involve being taken there by train or bus or car, we had to make a cart to take all our equipment with us.

This was a box put on bicycle wheels with ropes attached at the front and back, and the whole troupe would then pull this along the roads until we reached our destination, which in some cases was twenty three miles there and back. We did not seem to mind this, and it was probably part of the adventure to us.

At least we became self sufficient, and did not rely on parents or anyone to take us. In retrospect it was probably very good training for the life that was ahead for many of those boys when they went into the forces.

I was very jealous of some of the other boys who had sheath knives in leather cases. I could not afford one to buy, but I found an old rusty carving knife and cleaned it and rubbed it on sandstone until it was the right shape, then bound the handle with string and from a piece of old leather I also found, I made a sheath for it.

I was very proud of this, and to my deep satisfaction found that this was the biggest knife anyone in the troupe had, and it was the only one big enough to cut a loaf of bread!

One thing I remember during those days was walking down the road to the shops with my mother, we would always stop at the War Memorial Cross in the middle of the road called Broadway, and look at the name of George Baron. My mother had been engaged to him before the First World War, and he was tragically killed in France with so many others from the same town. I have a picture of my mother when she was young, and in this she is wearing a locket with a picture of George on it, I don't think she ever forgot him, even after marrying my father. This War Memorial Cross has now been moved to the back of St. Anne's Church in Royton.

I gave all my earnings from my various jobs to my mother, and she would give me one penny in the shilling back for pocket money. This enabled me to be able to go to the cinema perhaps once a week, at the Imperial Theatre or the Pavilion in Royton, which cost three pence. These cinemas were both owned by the same person, a man called Mr. Cheatham, and on occasions when the film broke down, all the boys would chant "Cheatham by name, Cheat'em by nature, Cheat'em on land and Cheat'em on water." Then he would come out and threaten to close the cinema unless we behaved.

My mother and father were still both unemployed as most people were at that time; we were an average northern family. We all wore clogs. My mother wore a shawl, as did most women then, a plain one during the week and a bright one for Sundays. They were an extremely useful garment, as they kept her warm during the day, were used as a bed cover at night, and were used by all the women as a sling to carry a baby around, an old idea of the modern baby carrier.

During the time I was delivering newspapers, someone told the means test people that I was doing this and receiving 4s.6d a week for this, so they told Dad that they would have to deduct this from his money, and instead of receiving 16s.00d a week for a family of six, he now only received 12s.00d. He was also told that should I give up my job, the money would not go up to 16s.00d again but would remain at 12s.00d, so I was forced to keep doing this job. Life seemed very hard in those days, but I think it prepared me for the rough times that lay ahead of me.

* * *

CHAPTER THREE

Starting work

I now came to a period of change in my life. I had to leave the Church Choir, as my voice was breaking, but I was quite relieved about this, as I had not been enjoying it for some time. It also came to school leaving time. I had enjoyed schooling, as I was near the top in most of the important subjects, but of course could not attend grammar school, my parents not having the money to keep me there, and the headmaster said how disappointed he was about this, but understood how things were, as most families were in the same position.

So at the age of 14 it was time to seek employment out of necessity. Like every other boy I wore short trousers at school, we all wore them until we were about fourteen, then most would have long trousers to start work. Unfortunately when I left school, Mam could not afford the price of a new pair of long trousers, but she managed to buy a pair of bib and brace overalls for me. I was nearly sixteen before I had any proper trousers, and at times this was very embarrassing, but I was not the only one in this predicament there being many families who could not afford extra clothes for their children starting work. Most lads at that time would spend months or even years searching for work, but I was lucky (or not!) in getting one within a week of leaving school. It was a terrible job, in a works producing springs for the interiors of car seats and beds. These springs had hessian sacking in between and I was given some sacking 6 feet wide in a long roll, and a large pair of scissors? The sacking was marked out in sections, 6 inches by 2 inches, and it was my job to cut this sacking into thousands of sections 6 by 2. When one piece of sacking was finished, I had to start another, and by the end of the first morning my hands were red raw and blistered, and they stayed like that until I left that job three months later. It was 48 hours a week and the wage was 7s.6d. I was very relieved to leave this after three months for a better job! I became a fettler in a brass foundry in Oldham, producing the brass parts for meters and covers. I was paid piecework and could then make about 12s.6d a week. It was a filthy dirty job, grinding the articles which came from the mould shop, some only small screws, and in grinding these on a wheel it nearly always took most of my fingernails off with it. The moulds were in black sand, and everything was so dirty, it became ingrained in my hands. There were no washing facilities at places of work then, so we all had to go home in that dirty state.

I was just past 15 years-old, when my father heard of a job as an apprentice panel beater at a coachbuilder in Morhey Street, Oldham. I immediately went there, and was lucky enough to get the job. That was an interesting job, a new chassis would come in and the body builders would build a frame round it and the panel beaters would shape the aluminium or steel to exactly fit the woodwork. Then away to the paint shop it would go to be either painted or sprayed, then to the fitting out shop to be fitted with carpets, seats and windows etc. finishing up as a beautifully finished coach or car etc. It was a very satisfying profession.

However, as satisfying as it was, I had always harboured the idea of being a surgeon, and it was with this in mind, I decided to go to night school to further my education, not having had the opportunity to this in my other jobs.

I duly enrolled at night school, but two weeks later the manager of the coach building company came to me in the workshop and said, "I hear you have started night school." I stuck my chest out and answered very proudly "Yes sir." But then the astounding reply came, "You can either work for me or go to night school, but not both, as you will not be available for overtime when I want it. You make your mind up what you want to do and let me know." There was only one answer of course, and so ended my ambition to further my education, and any thought of a medical career ended there and then. However I stayed there because it was a very satisfying and creative job.

As I have said before, times were very hard in the 1920s and early 1930s and every morning about twenty men would line up outside the offices in case someone did not turn up or was fired. There was so much unemployment. At the slightest sign of trouble or bad work one was fired and would be replaced in two minutes. The manager even had two body guards who when ordered would floor a man and then throw him out. I wonder what would happen if they did that now. All sorts of legal cases would be brought and compensation paid.

Being the youngest apprentice I had all sorts of duties to carry out apart from panel beating, like brewing tea and running errands. One duty involved going to the house of one of the men who lived not far away, and wait while his wife made tea and cut a piece of cake for him. It was never ready so she always made me sit down while I waited. She was always in a dressing gown and every day the ties came loose. Being very naïve, I did not grasp the significance of this until a few years later and by that time I was in the army. Did I miss something in my education then?

During my time in this job, I met some very interesting people. Two such people had the peculiarity of having no surnames. One was called Robin O'Kitsus and the other Tom O'Jammie. When I asked them what were their real names, it seemed that where they came from they took the name of their father, therefore Robin was out of Christopher, and Tom was out of James. In that part of the country in Northern England for centuries they had no surnames at all. Edgar Tasker was another very interesting chap, although he was then nearly eighty years of age, he still worked in the body-building workshop, though he had served his apprenticeship as a wheelwright. The place he started at in Manchester made horse drawn carriages. For the first two years there he was called number one boy, which involved starting at six in the morning, getting down into a pit when a full tree trunk would be put over him, and number two boy would get on top of the tree, and between them they would wield a two handed saw to saw the tree into planks. You can imagine what it would be like down that pit with saw dust falling on you all day. However after two years he became number two boy, then he was on top, and for another two years he spent sawing tree trunks from the top of the pit. So that was four years doing nothing but saw trees into planks. But after that he started the job of becoming a proper wheelwright, and he said that he could tell one kind of wood from another blindfolded after handling the tree trunks for four years. He really was a master craftsman. Everything he did was perfect. In my opinion he should have been given work on public places such as a Church or Public building where his work would have been preserved and seen for hundreds of years, it was so good.

The blacksmith who was called Sailor Tom by everyone because he had been a sailor previously, could also tell us such interesting things about his life. He had served in four mast sailing ships, and had finished in steamships. During our lunch break he would tell us some of his experiences around the world, and as none of us had ever been outside Lancashire, they were enthralling for us. Some were funny, some gruesome, and some spicy. However, when he left the sea and married, the only job he could find was in Salford, about eight miles away from where he was living. He had to start work at 6.0am and finished at 6.0pm. There was no break for lunch in those days, so he had to work a 12 hour shift. He had no transport and had to walk to work. This involved leaving home at 4.0am and it was downhill all the way to work, but after 12 hours hard graft he then had to walk uphill all the way back home, which took him about three hours, not arriving home until 9.0pm. It only gave him time to have a meal before going to bed, to get up at 4.0am again. Times were hard in my youth, but even harder for him.

Another person I recall was a young red headed lady in the office, and occasionally she would have to come out to see people or bring papers round. It was one Christmas that she came out with some papers and the boys in the body shop grabbed her and tied her to a chair, putting a piece of mistletoe on her head, so that for a couple of hours she had to endure everyone who passed by kissing her. She was getting redder and redder, and when eventually we released her she came up and kicked some of us, including myself. It served us right. No one would dare do that kind of thing now.

We also had a "knocker up man". He operated because most people could not afford a clock. He would start work very early in the morning, and from a list of the houses and the time each household wished to be woken he would begin by rattling on their windows with a long pole which had wires attached on the end, and would not stop until someone appeared at the window. When he finished his round he would then go round the streets and with the other end of his long pole he would turn off all the gas lamps. Each mill or workshop in the area had a steam siren all of which had different sounds, and every morning each steam clock would sound in sequence at the allotted time, one siren every quarter hour, and everyone would know when to leave for work. At night the Town Church would ring a bell for one minute at ten o'clock, this was called "The Nowstir Bell", telling everyone who was away from home to "now stir thiself, it's time for bed".

It was at this time that we moved to High Barn Street, near the centre of Royton. I vividly remember this move, as my father had borrowed a handcart from Mr. Smethurst the plumber, in which we piled all our possessions. It measured about 3 feet by 2 feet and it cost us sixpence to hire. Everything went in it including furniture, crockery and clothes, then with great excitement we pushed it to Highbarn Street in Royton. It was called "Flitting" then, not moving, and to be able to put everything for a family of six into one small handcart proves it was not a materialistic society then. This was the first full house we had ever lived in, four full rooms all to ourselves. I think the only reason we could afford it, was because it was so dark. Across the narrow street from us was the five-storey building of the Royton Spinning Company mill. We shared the back yard and lavatory with three other families. It was in this house that I remember having a terrible argument with my brother Ernest. I cannot remember what it was about, but he ran from me into the house and locked the door. I was so incensed that I grabbed an axe lying on the ground nearby and started to chop the door down, but Mam came home just in time to put a stop to it, and put us well and truly in our place. I think I have kept my temper under control since then.

*

In June 1939 I was 17 years-old, and had been an apprentice panel beater for two years. A panel beater in those days was far removed from the description of panel beater now. It involved making every thing by hand, from coaches, cars, ambulances, and aircraft skins, by shaping the metal by beating and wheeling.

By June 1939 everyone was sure that a war was imminent, and giving it very careful thought I came to the conclusion, as so many other young men did, that it was my duty to be prepared to fight for my country and people. Having made this decision, I joined the Territorial Army unit in Oldham, which was a Royal Tank Regiment unit. We trained once a week, mainly about tank procedures, tank engines, tank guns and radios, and wireless telegraphy. The Regiment at that time had only two tanks, and these were out of date and useless in modern warfare, but at least we were preparing.

I was still a boy scout and had arranged to go camping with them for the last week in August, to a place called Scawby near Scarborough. It was arranged on my suggestion that we would go by train from Royton to Scarborough. Because in the past certain ones of the troupe had always been late, it was arranged that we would have a block booking and anyone who was late would be left behind. Yes, guess what!! I was the only one late, so I had to run home, get on my rusty old bicycle with my pack on my back, and ride the 110 miles to camp.

* * *

CHAPTER FOUR

Outbreak of war

We all enjoyed the camp, but on the evening of the 1st September 1939 we heard a report on the radio that all reservists and Territorial members had to report to their units by the 3rd September. So the next morning I got my kit and mounted my rusty bike and rode to Scarborough railway station, where I explained to the station master that I was booked on a block ticket for the next day. He said "Get on the train lad, I will telephone ahead so that you will have no trouble", so I got home on the 2nd September.

On the morning of the 3rd September, in my full uniform and with my kit, I was ready to go and my mother kissed me. She had never kissed me before and has never kissed me since. So now when the anniversary of the outbreak of war comes round, I remember my one and only kiss from my mother. I was a very shy person, so on that morning I went the back way to report to my unit, so that I would not be seen. I went up Star Brew, then followed the railway line towards the gasworks, went over a stile and across the fields to Oldham Edge, and on to the Oldham Drill Hall where I signed in.

Most of my workmates used their "Reserved Occupation" status to avoid the call up. Some actually said it was silly to go because panel beaters would be in great demand during the war and would be able to demand a substantial wage for making aeroplane parts. However I have to record that one of these men was killed by a bus in the blackout, so it did not save him by staying at home.

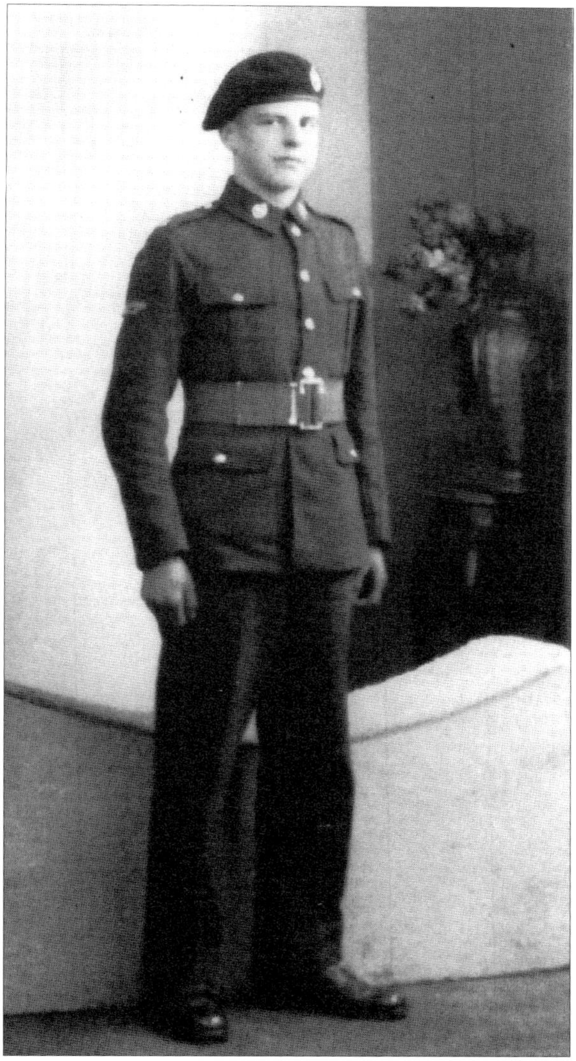

As a raw recruit

From Oldham Drill Hall we were marched up to Lees about four miles away, to Further Hey Mill, an old cotton mill that had closed a long time ago. On arrival I was issued with a ground sheet, a blanket, a lead coated plate and a basin, and then was shown to the space on the floor where I was to sleep. The man next to me was called Norman Bentley, and we became firm friends, though I never dreamt that in six years time I would marry his sister.

Life at Further Hey Mill was grim indeed, we all slept on the wooden floor and oil seeped out of the wood. So at night we would place our ground sheets down, then roll in our one blanket, use our boots for a pillow, and attempt to sleep. After the first night our commanding officer and medical officer came around and declared that the place was stinking and was short of ventilation so they immediately smashed every pane of glass to let in the fresh air. It was left in this state all winter, and if you have heard of the saying "Curse like a trooper", you can understand why. The showers and washing facilities, such as they were, were outside, as were the toilets, and they had no doors and not even a roof. The food was also very basic. Breakfast was a piece of boiled bacon, two slices of bread and a basin of tea. There was no such luxury of milk. Lunch was a ladle of stew and one slice of bread and a basin of tea. Supper was two slices of bread with jam, and the usual basin of tea. This menu was exactly the same for seven months. Of course we had time off from training and P.T. to use as we decided! We had washing to do, brasses to clean, boots to clean etc. However, we could occasionally get into town, and Norman and I went into Oldham, and it was there that I was introduced to Pubs and beer, bearing in mind that I was then still only seventeen years old.

I discovered that the main reason he took me with him, was that he smoked and in order to do this and afford beer as well, he could borrow from me for a pint or two, but he never did pay me back. He still owed me this money when he died in 1979, and a few other people said the same thing! Maybe when we all meet in the Tankman's Heaven he will be waiting there with my money in one hand and a pint of beer in the other. He was always forgiven his sins though as he was a brilliant pianist and musician. So when in town, if I had sixpence, which was enough for two half pints, he would find a pub with a piano, I would buy the two half pints of beer, and he would play, then people would buy us more drinks, it was so easy.

During the first three or four months, the commanding officer insisted on trying to knock the civilian attitude out of us. Once a week he would get us all, including officers, in two ranks facing each other. Boxing gloves were brought out and we fought the man facing us. Almost every time I seemed to get a big chap opposite me and I was knocked almost senseless. Also each week we ran two or three miles in full uniform, arriving back almost dead with fatigue.

Our pay was two shillings a day, and out of that I allowed one shilling to be paid to my mother at home, as they were still in dire straights. Two shillings were deducted for barrack room damages, leaving only five shillings for everything else, including toothpaste, shoe polish, soap, Brasso and Blanco etc.

In 1939 the winter was cold in the extreme, it was freezing for weeks and the snow was about six feet deep. All the Regiment was employed every day carrying coal, food and medicines to a T.B. Hospital on the Yorkshire Moors. We dressed in everything we could put on including boots and two pairs of socks, then over the boots we put about six sandbags and tied them on, to prevent skidding on the ice. Then we would walk in single file carrying our packs of goods, there and back. When that was over we helped to dig out railway trucks and carriages, which were snow bound at both ends of the railway tunnel, which runs under the Yorkshire Moors.

Occasionally when we got some leave, I would visit Norman's family and he would visit mine, so we got to know each others family very well.

Norman and I were transferred to the 41st Battalion the Royal Tank Regiment during the New Year of 1940; this Battalion was also in Oldham, but at the other side of town. Together we had many adventures and experiences, including two weeks inside the army prison for getting back to Barracks four hours late and a bit worse for wear!

We peeled potatoes and scrubbed cookhouse greasy pans etc. until 12.0 midnight for fourteen nights. It could all have been avoided, because I said we could climb over the wall to get in, but Norman said we could just walk inside pretending to be on duty. We tried this but found the Sergeant Major's dirty great paw on our shoulders, and no excuses, so we learned the hard way.

In March I was sent to the Royal Tank Regiment HQ in Bovingdon, Dorset, to take a Radio Operator instructors course, lasting three months. I had never been South before, and was amazed at some of the things I saw, especially the schools, which seemed to me to be beautiful buildings, with playgrounds, rugby fields and gymnasiums. I had never seen anything like it in the North, and compared the equipment these schools had with the one football the whole school shared at St. Anne's. The boys used it for football, and the girls used it for netball. However, we could not use it for football if we wore clogs. In my thinking it seemed that the country had been divided, with all the money for education going to the south and not very much to the north.

After arriving at Bovingdon to join my class, I discovered that it consisted mainly of officers from Captain downwards. We had Captains, Lieutenants, Staff Sergeants, Sergeants, Corporals, and then me the lowest of the low a mere trooper. I got very embarrassed especially in the teacher training exercises, as I had to get up in front of everyone and deliver a lecture. I was still only eighteen and a mere Trooper. It was a very good course, but when I think back on it, it seems so antiquated when compared with the equipment that is around now. Eventually I did pass out with flying colours. I could build a radio transmitter, and in Radio Telegraphy could send and receive Morse code at thirty words a minute this proving to be very advantageous to me. With this skill I could tune into Reuters, and get all the news at least a week before it was in

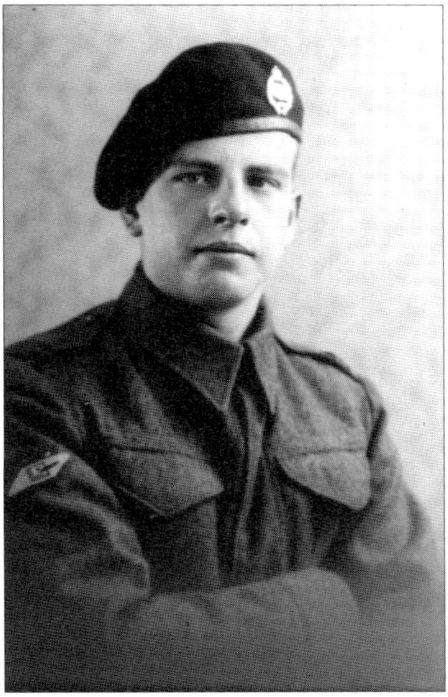

1940

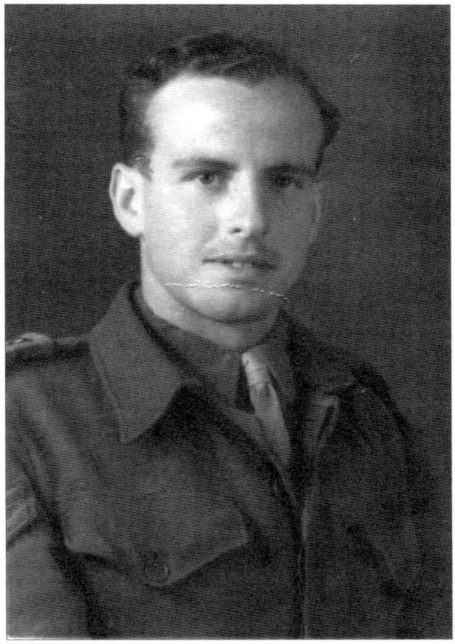

1945

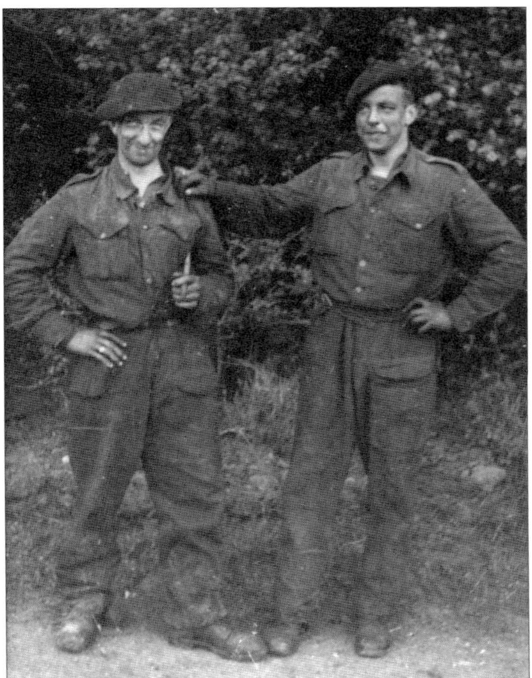

Jimmy Jackson and self in camp near Canterbury, 1942

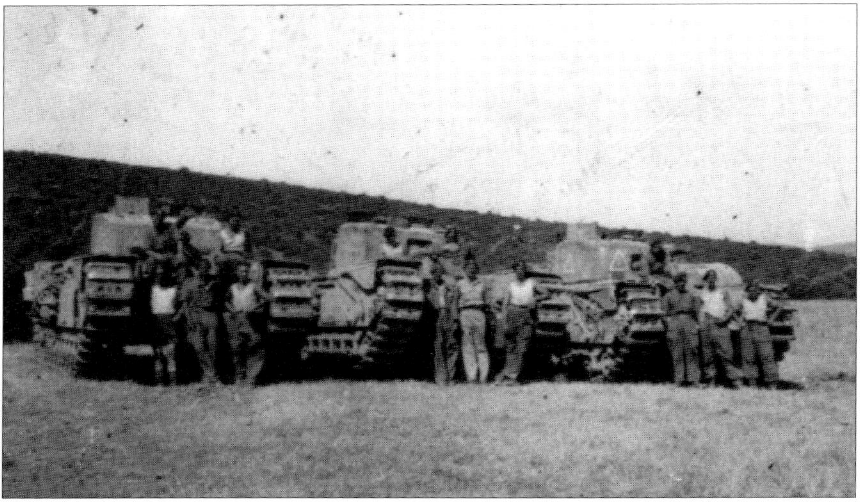

No 4 Troop; A Squadron 51 A.T.R. Africa

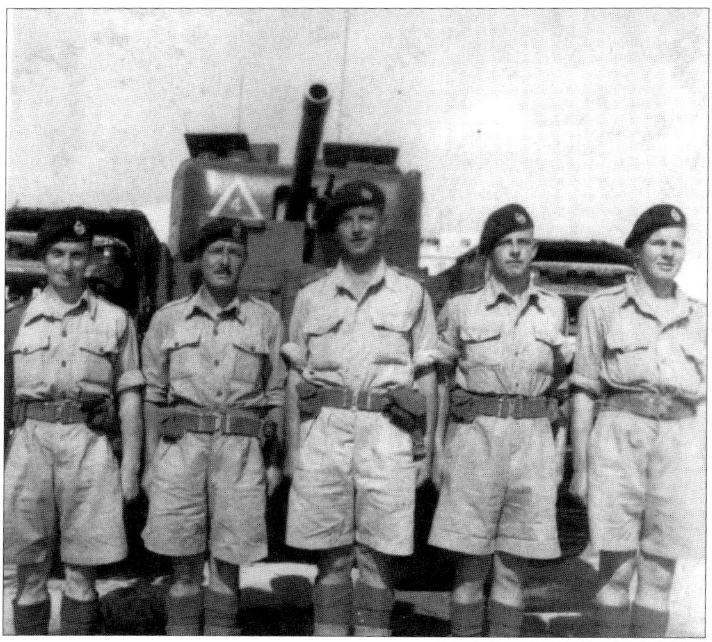

"Ardent" Tunisian victory march 1943
Left to right: Jimmy Jackson, driver; D. De Groot, OP; Fred Hartley, Commander; F. Ashworth, Turret Gunner; Bob Cottam, co-driver

the newspapers or on the radio. I also passed on the Aldis Lamp at twelve words a minute, at six words a minute in Semaphore. There were many other procedures to learn including all about batteries etc, so that I had knowledge of all Army Radio Procedures.

On returning to my regiment I was congratulated by my commanding officer, but he also told me that I was being transferred to another regiment the 51st in two weeks time. I was very disappointed, as I had made many friends, and it meant starting all over again. However, there was nothing I could do about it, and when the time came, about twenty of us set off in a truck for Catterick, in Yorkshire. I did find out that the reason for my transfer was my age; we were all only eighteen and my old regiment was going abroad and so we were transferred.

Eventually we arrived at our destination, not as we thought at Catterick Camp, but in the middle of Catterick Moor, miles from anywhere.

We were under canvas, and from the day we arrived, we had to stand to one hour before dawn every single day, that meant standing to at 4.0am during the summer. Our only weapons then were obsolete rifles from World War One. After a while some Austin ten Utilities and some plywood arrived, and we got the job of making mock up wooden tanks, this was so that in the event of spy planes coming over, it would appear that we were well armed.

However, eventually the new Churchill tanks started to arrive, but as they were a completely new model, they had their faults, and as a new regiment we were given the task of rectifying them.

We were soon moved to the North East coast near Holy Island. Here we had three jobs, and the only way I can explain it, is that it was three tiered. The first job being to act as pillbox sentries on the beach, and if the Germans invaded we were instructed to hold them as long as possible. If we were overwhelmed we were to fall back two miles to the Austin Utilities, which were equipped with machine guns, and again we were to harass and hold them off as long as possible. If this did not deter them, we had then to fall back a further ten miles inland to where the few tanks we had were hidden in a wood. We had then to crew these, attack the enemy and hope to push them back to the sea. But as we all know now, they never came thank goodness, as the country at that time was so ill prepared.

One amusing thing happened when we were on sentry duty in the pillboxes on the beach. We had set up a camp kitchen, and every day we had the same meal, which was stew! So many complained about it when the colonel came round one day, that he went to the cook and ordered him to put dumplings in it. He obeyed this order and put in the dumplings, only to find that a few minutes later the dumplings had multiplied in size, had pushed off the lid of the saucepan and everything poured over the sides like some live monster. So for the remainder of our stay we continued with stew without dumplings.

Our next move was down to Yorkshire near to Pocklington a small town not far from York. The next week we were marched to the local cinema, and once we were all settled inside the Commanding Officer climbed onto the stage in front of the screen and said, "We are now going into serious training and it is going to be rough. I have had a letter from the War Office offering me ATS women to work in the office, cook house and transport etc. but I have refused. Stating that I believe that if a man needs a woman to help him to soldier, then I do not need him in this regiment. So if any man of any rank thinks differently they need only to step forward and they will be transferred without any questions asked. Those who do not step forward I will assume they are of my opinion."

No one stepped forward in the next ten minutes, and he said, "Right then, so from now on we will prepare for the real thing. In war you will be tired and hungry, cold and uncomfortable and frightened. I do not know how to make you frightened, but I do know how to make you cold and uncomfortable, tired and hungry, and I will bloody well do so, for the benefit of us all. Dismiss." And he kept his word; he made life hellish. It was from here I went to Lulworth again to take a gunnery course, which I passed, then to another course in the Drill Hall in Newcastle on Tyne.

*

It was in Newcastle that I met a nice young lady called Nancy, she lived not far from Newcastle in Jesmond Dean, a very upper class area, but she was my undoing! I was on duty one night as sentry at the entrance to the drill hall, when she arrived with some chocolates. It started to rain and Nancy squeezed in behind me in the sentry box. It was very intimate with the closeness and warmth of our two bodies, but along came the duty officer, and as he was asking me if all was well, Nancy burst out laughing. That meant another two weeks inside for me, just my luck! Eventually back to Pocklington I went.

In a tank crew every man must be trained to do every job in the tank. So it was near Pocklington that I did my driving courses. The first week I was given a motorcycle, and by the end of the week I had passed out on the theory and practical course of the motorcycle. After that came vehicles up to three tons, then heavy vehicles including tank transporters, these had sixteen gears with an intermediate gear making thirty-two gears in all. In those days all gearboxes were crash boxes. After that came the track vehicles, starting with the smallest and graduating to the largest which were our own tanks. I am very pleased to say that I passed out in them all.

We eventually received the remainder of our tanks making us at long last a fully equipped regiment. This meant that we were now put on full war footing, and each crew lived together, eating, working and sleeping by the tank no matter what rank they were, and everyone took their turn to cook. We had no buildings or barracks, not even a tent, only a piece of tarpaulin, which was fastened to the tank for a makeshift shelter. It was fastened about five feet from the ground, then stones were put on the bottom to anchor it, and we all slept under this. For the remainder of the war no matter where we landed up, we lived like this in the open air, in freezing cold winter or the heat of summer, we never had a barracks or tents to call home.

Owing to my course on Radio Procedures at Bovingdon, I was the most advanced operative in the regiment, and so was immediately claimed by the colonel as his operator.

In a Churchill Tank at that time there were six transmitters and six receivers, a complete intercom to all the crew, and a telephone situated at the rear of the tank in a metal box, which is used by the infantry to contact the colonel and crew. Being the Colonel's tank the radio had to be attended at all times 24 hours a day, and if you were the one on duty you could not take the headphones off in case an urgent message came through. All the operators took their turn, and one night when I was on duty, it was about 3.0 o'clock in the morning, I had to obey a call of nature. As my headphones tied me to the tank, I could not get out to go to the lavatory, and during war times to take the headphones off was a dereliction of duty punishable by death. So the only thing to do was to climb out of the turret still with my headphones on, go to the side of the tank where I knew the crew were not sleeping, whereupon I relieved myself. To my horror I heard the voice of the Colonel splutter and say, "Is it raining?" I replied, "Sorry Sir, I did not expect anyone to be sleeping this side." And he said, "Do you mean to say you have actually pissed on me?" I apologised once more, but a week later I was transferred to number four troupe, which was one of the fighting troupes. I became operator to Lieutenant Fred Hartley, who was nicknamed Jam, as he was a member of the famous family of Hartley's Jams. I found out later that from then on the Colonel slept on the same side as the crew!

We received orders to move to the shores of Loch Fyne in

Scotland, and were moved there by train. This proved a difficult task, as Churchill Tanks are the largest heavy tanks and overhung the flat trucks. However, we eventually managed to get them on and moved up to arrive at a station called Arrechar. Having unloaded the tanks with great difficulty, we moved over the steep hills up a road called Rest And Be Thankful! Yes it is true that was the name of the road and as far as I know it is still there.

It proved quite a hazard going over the top of hills and down into Loch Fyne, but we made it and there we met up with the Commandos, with whom we trained for the next few months. Each morning we would load the tanks on to landing craft, three tanks to a ship, sail out about a mile, turn round and attack the shore, which the Commandos were to defend. We were almost sure that we had been picked to cross the Channel and land in France. After a few weeks of very hectic training there, I was very pleased I was not in the Commandos. They were taken out into the country in trucks for about thirty miles nearly every morning, and without the trucks slowing down they had to jump off, roll over with their full kit on, then hike thirty miles back before doing their normal days training.

After finishing this training at Loch Fyne, we were then moved down to South West Wales, in Pembrokeshire. Here there was a live ammunition tank range, where we trained with the guns. In doing so we had squadron against squadron using live ammunition, though thankfully not armour piercing shells! This was as close as they could get us to real active service.

It was not long before we were off again, this time on tank transporters up to Sherwood Forest. This enabled us to train in a forest area where we learnt to hide the tanks in the foliage, and we were there for quite a while. However we did manage to get out for the occasional evening in Worksop. Also, if we were static for any length of time, we managed to get some leave, and I had a weeks leave to go home during this time.

Whenever we had to move from one area to another, we had to do this at night, for the obvious reason that we would not be observed by any enemy or spies that might be around. It was not long after my leave that we were told to prepare for an exercise involving many thousands of men and troops including Canadian Infantry. Our eventual target was a small wood near the town of Aylsham in Kent, about 180 miles away from where we were. This was the first time that the public would have seen these tanks, and we were a bit apprehensive as they were such big heavy vehicles they could do a lot of damage. This exercise lasted for about five weeks, giving the Generals experience in the movement of vast numbers of troops, the communications systems, and even the transport delivery system.

My tank crew consisted of Fred Hartley as commander, Bob Brotherton as operator, who before the war had been assistant Manager of the Edinburgh Opera House. Jimmy Jackson the driver, Bob Cottam who was the co-driver, with whom I became good friends, he had been the assistant manager of a snuff works in Kendal, and then myself as the turret gunner. It was during this exercise that we found ourselves in the middle of Windsor Great Park, and what a shock the groundsmen must have had the next morning, when they found big tank tracks dug right across the middle of the beautiful lawns, though at the time we had no idea we were in the King's grounds, and it must have taken months if not years to correct the damage.

We were just about to pat ourselves on the back for everything going to plan when going through the town of Chalfont St. Peter we started having engine trouble. We stopped near the railway station and worked through the night trying to repair the trouble, but to no avail. We contacted headquarters, and they asked us to get off the road if possible, to avoid a traffic jam when dawn came. We managed to get off the road by slowly moving down into the railway yard. We were by then all covered in thick black engine oil and were exhausted, so we all fell asleep on top of the engine deck. The next morning was Saturday, and we cleaned ourselves up and waited for our fitters to arrive. However, we received a radio message to the effect that they could not get to us that day, but we would have to wait five days to be rescued. So making sure that someone was always on guard, we went to the Railway Hotel about 200 yards away, and when the landlady found out who we were she generously declared that she would provide us with all our meals at the pub during the time we had to wait there. We of course immediately voted her our No.1 pin-up.

During Saturday afternoon a big chauffeur driven car arrived, and out stepped the Commanding Officer of all the Home Guard in that area. He asked if he could have permission to bring about five hundred of his troops to see the tank, as none of them had seen one before, and could we also instruct them on how they could stop an enemy tank if any came their way. We agreed to this, thinking it would relieve our boredom.

Sunday morning after church parade they all marched down to the railway yard, and we allowed them to climb into the tank to see what they would be up against, and to ask any questions. They then assembled to parade back to where they had come from, when along came the CO's daughter. I happened to be nearest, and he asked if I would kindly let her see inside. I agreed of course, and showed her how to climb onto the tank, into the turret and so inside. I climbed in after her to explain how things worked. After a few minutes I heard her father shout out to me, and I climbed up into the turret cupola to see what he wanted. As I conversed with him, I was astounded to feel two hands round me. You can imagine my feelings trying to talk to a commanding officer, when his daughter is out of sight behaving in a most disturbing manner. However we tank men are made of stern stuff, and when I could, I remonstrated with her saying that well brought up young ladies did not do that kind of thing to a soldier, when said soldier is talking to Daddy!

We enjoyed the following four days, in good company and enjoying good meals provided by the landlady of the pub. We were sorry when at last the tank was repaired and we rejoined our squadron in the wood near Aylesham.

We were then told of the reason for our move to Kent. Army Intelligence had been told that the Germans were assembling a large army to attack that summer on the South East Corner of England.

Luckily they never got to invade as we were still unprepared and under fully armed.

If they did invade, our role was to go over the cliffs at Deal in the East, in an attempt to cut them off from supplies and reinforcements. Another surprise defence against them was that numerous pipes had been laid under the Channel around the South East Coast, and a mixture of oil and petrol would be pumped through them to about five miles out in the Channel. This mixture would float to the surface and would be ignited setting fire to anything in the area.

Our squadron had to be ready at all times, and in the wood we were in, a concrete tank base had been made to enable us to make a quick get away if necessary. This was in early 1942, we were a fully trained unit and we were pretty certain that we would be in the invasion fleet when the time came.

In the meantime, my friends and myself were able to get out and we visited Canterbury, and Dover, which were only a few miles away. Once when we were in Dover, the German guns in Calais, France started shelling the town, and we all had to take cover in the passages, which had been dug into the white cliffs. It was in these tunnels that we came across a restaurant and it appeared that only Generals and Admirals were the clientele, however, we decided to order a meal, and noticed we were getting black looks from everyone, but we carried on and had a thoroughly good time.

Aylesham was only a mile away from where we were stationed, and we had many a good time there. One morning at about 6.0am I was trying to sneak back into camp, when I ran into squadron Sergeant Major Richardson. I must tell you a bit about him. He was the strictest disciplinarian I have ever met, but he was so decent, that he would punish a man rather than put him on a charge, and this kept his record sheet clear. On one occasion he even dismissed the Colonel's parade at 9.0 o'clock because the colonel was one minute late, telling him that he ordered the parade for 9.0o'clock not one minute past.

Having been confronted by him, I was told that I was just in time! He said that he wanted a hole digging 6 feet by 6 feet by 6 feet immediately, and it took me until 9.0 pm that evening before I had finished it. Having measured it to make sure the measurements were correct, he then told me to fill it in again, and that took me another four hours. I then slept very well for the rest of the night.

When eventually we were posted overseas, Sergeant Major Richardson was told that he was too old to go with us, and as a mark of our respect and thanks, we all had a collection and bought him and his wife a lovely silver rose bowl.

During our time in the woods, General Montgomery was in charge of that area at the time, and once inspected us.

On hearing that the 41st Regiment was in Folkestone a friend and myself went there to see how Norman Bentley was faring. We found him to be training with Matilda tanks, which had a million watt light on the turret, this idea was to attack at night blinding the enemy, but for some reason it was never used. We left Norman and his company, wishing them luck and not expecting to see them again for a long time. We were then moved to the South Downs and after manoeuvres, we ran into his squadron, but Norman was not around at that time, so I helped myself to his tea, sugar and milk powder, and we had a brew up. He never did forgive me when he found out!

Another time I met him at the Thomas a Becket public house in Worthing, and as we were having a drink, two good looking girls came in and we chatted them up for a couple of hours. To our chagrin we then found out they were Lesbians; you could have knocked us down with a feather! Just our luck!

Another little escapade I must tell you about was when I was out with two of my friends, when we bumped into Norman in a pub in Worthing, and we had eventually run short of money. We only had sixpence between us, and on leaving the pub a bit worse for wear we came upon a place selling sandwiches, which was just closing. So we negotiated with him and bought all his left over sandwiches for our sixpence, and we then went round Worthing selling these sandwiches at three pence each. After which we returned to the pub for more to drink! We left Norman and set off for our camp, taking our boots off because they made a noise, and hung them round our necks. We arrived at our squadron to find that the sentry was another friend, Tommy Bennett,we fooled around with him and took his sub machine gun from him, only to be caught by the Orderly Officer. We all got two weeks inside, although the offence of taking a man's arms from him in war time was really punishable by death, so we considered ourselves lucky in the circumstances.

One of my friends named Peter, who was a very small person, was a tank driver, and had to have all the controls altered to fit him. We went to a dance one night in Worthing and at this event there were many Canadian Infantry men, they were mostly big strapping and rough looking types. The evening came to a close and the National Anthem was played and everyone stood to attention except a group of these French Canadians. So Peter when he saw this went over to them and asked them to stand up. I could not hear what was said, but Peter suddenly lashed out and hit the biggest of these men so hard he floored him and he was unconscious. It was so unlike Peter he was such an amiable chap, but I found out that in action he was ruthless. It seemed such an unlikely thing to do from such a mild mannered person, who had been brought up by his mother and her two sisters, his Aunts, and no men at all in the family. He was like a nineteenth century gentleman or something from the Scarlet Pimpernel, as he would always start a question by saying, "Pray tell me…" Not as we others would say, "What is that….". Nevertheless he was a fine chap.

We stayed in Worthing for a few months, and there were many regiments of tanks and infantry around, as it was thought that if an invasion materialised, we would all be waiting for them. During this lull in proceedings, life had to carry on and leave was given and sports and recreations were carried on. Football and Rugby matches were arranged and many other sports including cross-country running, in which I was always the Squadron representative.

Many units took part with about fifty runners over a course of fifteen miles, and one by one most of them dropped out, leaving three runners, one of which was myself. I thought I would at least get a place, when suddenly out of the blue another runner flew past us and vanished into the distance to finish first. I did manage to finish third, and found out that the winner had represented England in the Olympic Games just before the war. I suppose it was no disgrace to come third to an Olympian.

* * *

CHAPTER FIVE

Embarkation and action

My turn came for leave, so off to Royton I went, and while I had been away my parents had moved house again. This time it was a semi detached council house, the first really respectable house they had since being married. They even had chickens in the back garden!

During this leave I bumped into a previous lady friend, so we went and had tea in a local café, and during the conversation she invited me to have lunch with her the following day at her house. I duly turned up at the arranged time and it was only then that she told me she had married, and that her husband worked twenty-six miles away and did not get home until 6.30 pm. We chatted about old times, and had an aperitif followed by a gorgeous lunch with wine, finished off by a brandy. Suddenly she started up, saying, "My goodness did you hear that? That is the noise of our old car, my husband must be early"

I immediately said "Lock both the front and the back doors and whichever he goes to he will have to knock to get in, you can then shout that you are coming, and in the meantime I will nip out of the other door." So this was what happened, as he knocked on the front door, I nipped out the back. I realised that I could not turn right as that would lead me to the front door, so to the left I was forced to go across the back lawn, over the low fence which I found was too high to stride over and a rusty nail caught on my trousers, and part of the fence attached itself to me. Then across next doors back lawn and up their drive and away, with part of the fence with me. The lady next door had seen me and leaned out shouting "Stop thief" I had to run like mad then which was rather difficult with seven inches of fencing attached to me. However I crossed her drive and out the gate trying to walk nonchantly down the road. I tore the piece of fencing off and threw it over a wall, some of my trousers going with it. It served me right for lunching with a married lady!

I visited Norman's family to let them know that I had seen him and that he was well, I also renewed my aquaintance with his sister Doreen. I also met one of my old workmates who had transferred to war work to avoid being called up. On the last night of my leave I met one of my friends from the Squadron, we had arranged to meet in a pub at Newton Heath in Manchester. We found that the pub was full of the ladies from the munitions works at Ferranti and we were the only two men there. The girls had a kitty of money from which all their drinks were being bought, and they included ours even though we had not donated to it. These ladies were hard working in a very dangerous occupation, and the salt of the Earth.

I went back to my Squadron, which was A squadron of the 51st Battalion of the Royal Tank Regiment. I had only been back a couple of days when orders came through that all tanks were to be taken for a full overhaul, and they were loaded onto tank transporters and away they went. All the personnel were then moved to the outskirts of Wivenhoe, a village near Colchester.

*

A couple of days later, Bob Cottam who was co-driver in my tank and I went to the Corn Exchange in the middle of Colchester, which was then the local dance hall. We got chatting to two young ladies who were friends, and danced with them. The young lady I was with was called Joan but I cannot remember the name of her friend, but after the war, Bob and this girl were married and they settled in Kendal.

Joan and I became very close friends, and whenever we arranged to meet, her father would deliver her to the meeting point in a Rolls Royce. I once went to her home, but her parents were in London at the time where they had another house, because her father worked in Whitehall. We had to walk there as there were no cars at that time, and it must have been about half a mile to walk up the drive. They must have been really wealthy, because although clothes were on ration at that time, only to be bought if you had enough coupons to spare, she always turned up in a new dress every time we met. Her father must have been high up in Whitehall, as she once asked me if I wanted to stay in the army, because if I wanted to get out her father could arrange for my demobilisation and would find me a position in London. Of course I could not do that, I would have considered myself a coward and would have been ashamed. I could have arranged to get out of the forces myself as I was an apprentice panel beater when I went in and panel beaters were wanted to make the skins of aircraft, and all through the war there was a shortage of these tradesmen so it could have been easy for me.

During the short time in Wivenhoe we all enjoyed ourselves then one morning at about 10.00 am, we all had to assemble in the large marquee, which was our dining tent. We all crowded in, and the commanding officer came in through the middle flap at the far end. He asked for a space to be made up the middle for him to walk through, this he did and said "As from now everyone is confined to camp, no-one is allowed to speak or write to anyone outside. Everyone to my left will be going on 48 hours leave at 12.00 noon, and when you return in two days, everyone on my right will do the same. This will be your embarkation leave, but you will all sign a form stating that you will not tell anyone, this includes your families and friends. If it is found that this information has been passed on, all these people will be arrested and put in isolation until a safe period has elapsed." I was to the left of the CO so at 12.00 noon loaded with everything I possessed, including a Thompson machine gun and a revolver all fully loaded with ammunition, I was on my way with half of the squadron to the railway station. This was all very awkward, as I had arranged to see Joan that night, and in no way was I allowed to contact her. I did hear a few months later that she had waited for over two hours for me, and she told her friend (Bob Cottam's girl) that she never wanted to see me again. That was the end of a beautiful friendship, as I never did see her again.

So there I was on the train to London, to change trains for Manchester. Unfortunately, owing to the disruption of travel and train times in those days I eventually only managed five hours at home, before starting back to arrive at camp before the 12 o'clock deadline. I managed it with less than half an hour to spare, and then the other half of the squadron went on their way to return before their deadline was up.

That night at about 9.0 pm we were all called to parade with all our kit. It was very dark, and after a roll call, when it was established that everyone was present, we were marched out of camp across the fields and country roads to Colchester Railway Station. There we found the Military Police, the Red Caps, waiting in two lines from the station door. All civilians had been barred from the area, and in single file we had to walk through the door, between the files of Red Caps to the only unlocked door on the train. This was to prevent anyone from absconding, or communicating with outsiders, they even had orders to shoot if it was necessary. All the blinds were down and we were not allowed to open them. The one open door was locked and the train moved off through the dark night.

Shortly after moving from the station, we were ordered to remove all our Tank Regiment uniforms, including our berets, as at that time, the Tank Regiment was the only Regiment to wear the black beret. We were then issued with Royal Artillery uniforms and headgear, including badges. The train continued on through the night, no one knew where we were headed, until eventually it stopped and the one door was again opened, allowing us to alight in single file. We then saw that we were at Liverpool docks, and opposite us was a large ship.

We then had to walk through the line of Red Caps once again from the train straight up the gangway and onto the ship, which was called the *Empire Pride*. She had been a cargo ship and had been converted into a troop carrier. The original three holds, one aft, one forward, and one amidships, had been converted into five decks, and we had to proceed down to these decks and find ourselves a space for a hammock. Once we were aboard, the ship cast off her moorings, and immediately put to sea, heading towards the Irish Sea, continuing north towards Glasgow. We met a convoy outside Glasgow, and we found out later that this convoy consisted of very fast ships.

We then headed out towards the Atlantic, and we were then each issued with a hammock and a blanket, but we found that there was not enough room on the bars to swing all the hammocks, even though they were slung head to toe like sardines, so the unlucky ones had to put their hammocks on the floor to sleep. In the middle of each deck was placed a large half-barrel, which was intended for those unfortunates who were seasick, and it was tough luck for those unlucky enough to be sleeping near the barrel!

The British Tommy is nothing if not resilient, and even in those conditions, could still find time to play tricks on each other. There was one trick played on those who wanted to use the primitive toilet facilities, which consisted of a trough with a horizontal pipe in front running the whole length of the deck. Down this trough at periodic intervals a wave of seawater ran down to wash it out. The jokers amongst us thought it was a great laugh to make little paper sailing boats, set light to them, and when a wave of water came, would sail them down underneath the bottoms of the men using these toilets. Of course there were no discreet curtains or anything, and this all happened in full view of everyone.

The deck I was on was five decks down, and having worked out that if we were torpedoed I would not have stood a chance; I volunteered on the second day at sea to help man the 12-pounder guns on deck.

I stayed on the open deck with the guns, even during the periods of rain and rough seas, until we eventually landed in Africa. Not only was it safer I thought, but it was also much cleaner and I was able to breathe fresh air instead of the odour of hundreds of men, in all states of cleanliness.

During the voyage, I saw lights on a distant land, and asked one of the crew if he knew where it was and he answered that it was America. After this sighting, the convoy turned completely around and sailed East back towards the Mediterranean Sea. It was during this time that the weather turned stormy, and large numbers of the men were seasick so badly, that they even contemplated suicide. These men were placed on the deck and nets placed over them which were nailed to the deck, to prevent them harming themselves. During one night we passed Gibraltar and continued into the Mediterranean. We then changed back into our own uniforms, even the colonel had been disguised. We were also told why there had been all this deception and the speed of the convoy. Army intelligence had found out that the Germans intended sending their tiger tanks to Africa, and the medium tanks that the British had there were not good enough to engage the German tigers, so my Regiment was rushed out. In reality the German tiger tank out gunned every allied tank, including our Churchills, their main gun was the 88mm, which in my opinion was the best and most feared gun of any nationality.

We proceeded east for another couple of days then in the dark we came to the shore. We were told it was Libya. We were ferried ashore, and then the ship left. That night we slept where we landed, then at daybreak we walked along for about two miles, and found that our tanks and equipment had also been landed. How I do not know, because where we landed there was only a beach. After each crew had found their own tank, and moved into the squadron area, we were ordered to put sheets over them. We had to load up with everything we needed including the full amount of ammunition, and be prepared to leave in 24 hours. Late the next day a full complement of tank transporters arrived, the tanks and all our possessions were loaded, and we also travelled on them. For those who have never seen a tank transporter, they are a large truck having ten wheels and a huge engine. Over the back thirty tons of concrete is loaded, simply to hold the wheels down to grip the ground, because of the weight of the trailers and tanks. The trailer has twenty-four wheels, the tank is chained on, and the trailer is attached to the transporter by a triangular towing bar.

We were then given a warning to be prepared for a long journey, as we would not be stopping for anything until we reached our destination. In fact we were on the move for three and a half days non-stop. There were many difficulties we had to overcome on this journey.

The diesel was delivered in jerry cans, these had to be passed to us from the delivery truck running alongside us, the empties then being passed back. Food and water for our crew and the two-man crew of the transporter came to us in the same way. Sleeping was a disaster, for there was nowhere to lie down. The only way we could manage this was to tie ourselves with rope to the front mudguards, one man each side and with bits of rag stuffed in our ears we managed a little rest.

The biggest trouble was dealing with the call of nature over these three days. To urinate was no trouble, but for the other it was a huge dilemma. To get around to this we had to go through the following performance. Each member of the crew in turn would take off his trousers and underpants, two ropes were tied round the chest, the other four men would take the strain while the man was lowered over to sit on the connecting triangular towing bar between the transporter and trailer. To look over your shoulder while sitting there was to see the fearsome sight of ten wheels pounding along with the terrific weight on them, and to ponder what would happen if you fell off. When you had finished you were pulled up again to find your trousers once more.

It was a wonder we were not all constipated for the whole journey. What a life for anyone, we wondered why we had joined!

Eventually after all this torment we arrived at our destination, which was simply a map reference. There were no buildings, and no roads, but this was our home for 24 hours. During that time we had the tanks unloaded with all our equipment and the transporters went back to where they came from. We then tried to get some rest after the terrible journey.

During the giving of our next orders we were told that we must always save at least two bullets for ourselves, in case we should fall into the hands of the Arabs.

We did manage to get some rest, although even this was interrupted by the usual spells of duty, as at all times two men of the crew had to be on guard, and this practice was carried out until the end of the war.

At this time my crew consisted of Fred Hartley, nickname Jam, as Commander, Dicky de Groot the operator, myself the turret gunner, Jimmy Jackson, the driver, and Bob Cottam the co-driver. The tank was named Ardent, and the other tanks in Four Troop were named Active and Aggressor.

There were five troops and the headquarters group making 18 tanks in all. Headquarters Troop also had two Daimler Dingos, these were armoured scout cars, which had five forward and five reverse gears. The whole group was called the fighting Echelon. We also had A,B,C & D Echelons. A Echelon was the group, which brought our supplies of food, water, ammunition etc. up to the squadron at night. The other echelons remained at a distance behind the lines, each with their respective duties.

At dusk we moved forward about three miles, which brought us to a range of hills and a position just at the rear of the Coldstream Guards Infantry Regiment.

There we had a briefing when we were told that the Coldstreams and us were to make a dawn attack starting at 5.0am the next morning. Our troop would be on the right where the hills were the steepest.

We were also told that we would be attacking an SS Panzer Grenadier Regiment. Our Regiment and the Coldstreams synchronized watches, and then tried to get a little rest.

At about 4.30am the next morning we moved forward to the Coldstream Guards positions. During the previous evening and during the night we had maintained strict radio silence, but on the very second of 5.0 o'clock, our C.O. broke the silence by coming on air and saying, "Squadron Advance".

As this was our first action, we were naturally very nervous. Fred Hartley (Jam) our tank commander was looking through his periscopes keeping a check on the route and also searching out targets, and then relaying this information down to me. I was also searching for targets through my telescope, which was a very powerful instrument and brought the enemy from a distance of 500 yards, looking near to 50 yards.

Then all hell was let loose. We destroyed numerous enemy positions and many of the men manning them. My tank was hit a few times, but we were lucky in that they were ricochets, and did not pierce our armour. Then I started having trouble with my Besa Machine Gun, it was sticking and then completely jammed. I tried everything to get it working again but to no avail. So on the intercom I told the co-driver Bob to get the Besa gun from the mounting in the front and to let me have it, and he could have my useless one! He did this and I eventually managed to get mine from its mounting, but it was so hot it burned through my gauntlets, and I received burns to the palms of my hands. It was during the hand over of these guns that I remember most clearly Bob Cotham's face being streaked with black oil and because of the extreme heat it was dripping off his nose. I fastened the other Besa in, and got it loaded and working. During this time we were hit about fifteen times, but they all bounced off, and we counted our lucky stars. We lived a charmed life that day. We found that one shot had penetrated about three inches, and had it gone another quarter of an inch it would have set off six hand grenades, which were just in front, and we would not have stood a chance. Things began to quieten down a bit, and eventually the S.S. Panzer Regiment surrendered to us.

When we rendezvoused in a small valley, we found that we had lost two tanks. They had been hit and set on fire and all the crew in both tanks were dead. One of the dead men had been my personal friend, the driver Joe Wilson. Half an hour later one of our tanks came rolling up and when it stopped I went over to it, climbed on to it and lifted the front flaps in order to speak to my friend Jack Harrison who had lived only two miles from me at home. He said that he could not get out, and I reached under him in order to pull him out, but my hand went straight inside his body as half of his buttocks had gone. We eventually got him out and he was put in a Jeep ambulance to be taken to first aid and then to hospital, where he was eventually invalided out.

When we came to rest we formed a laager; this name came from the South African Boers, which meant a fortified position. As night fell, we would fall back about half a mile, and one tank would be allocated to form the point. On a suitable piece of ground it would turn round to face the enemy positions, the next tank would park three or four yards back but to one side, then another tank would do the same on the other side. This was repeated until six tanks were in position on each side, making an arrowhead formation. The remaining tanks would fill in the back but facing away from the enemy making it into a triangle. This created a fort with most of the guns facing the enemy, but the rear ones covering our back. When the A Echelon was sighted, one of the rear facing tanks would reverse into the triangle making an entrance for them, and then would returned to seal the entrance again, while they dropped our supplies, the same in reverse on leaving. As I explained before, two men in each tank would always remain on guard, one in the turret with headset on and the other outside lay down with his ear to the ground to detect the noise of anyone approaching.

After the first battle, I realised that it was purely by luck that we survived the day as all the odds were against us. The SS Panzer Grenadiers were an elite regiment, and were experienced in warfare. We were attacking, which means we were in the open, but they were hidden. After that first engagement, one of our men spoke to one of the S.S. men who told him that they had thought it was impossible for any tank to climb the hills surrounding them. I think the Churchill Tank is the only one capable of this feat. It would go anywhere.

One little incident happened about two or three days after, which really surprised me. A Coldstream Guardsman who had been wounded, but who had just been found, was brought out on a stretcher to near my tank. On cutting his trousers off, it was found that both his legs were smashed, and one in particular was going gangrenous. When the first aid men saw this they pulled a small box from their pack and took maggots out from it, which they put on the gangrenous leg, then loosely bandaged it up, this was a lesson learnt from the First World War.

That was our first day in action, our baptism of fire, our introduction to the Germans, and our first casualties. There were many times similar to that first day. We operated with many different regiments and in many different areas. I remember vividly most of these battles, they are something memory does not dull and cannot be forgotten, but I sometimes remember them in the wrong order.

I found the reason for the jamming of my Besa gun was the verdigris on the rounds of ammunition, caused by the containers being split and the damp air getting in. When that night the A Echelon came round, the sergeant major brought his truck to the tank delivering our ammunition and asked me how many boxes I wanted. When he delivered the required amount onto the tank I noticed that about 6 boxes were split. I saw red, then grabbed my revolver and seriously threatened to shoot him, as this could have meant the death of us all if the gun had jammed again. The remainder of the crew came over, and calmed me down and eventually everything was sorted out. I was never offered bad ammunition again, but I mention this episode to illustrate the intensity of life at the front, and this was not an isolated one.

I am trying to convey just what it is like to go into battle in a tank, and explain about the crew and what a tank is like. Firstly the crew consisted of five men, who all wore rubber soled boots, and a tank suit. This suit was made of anti-inflammatory material for obvious reasons, and covered the whole body from the neck to the ankles and also to the wrists. It was zipped up from the legs to the neck, and there were two racks of tools on both shins, on the left knee and the front of each upper arm. On the right knee were a writing pad and pencil, and a revolver. When the suit is put on, a neck strap about an inch wide is then put on containing two microphones and strapped around the throat. Then goggles were put on. These were not ordinary goggles, as they had an apron of leather around them, the edges of which were bound with copper. This was pressed all round the face and head, leaving only the mouth and nostrils uncovered, thus providing very good protection against fire.

A pair of padded earphones was then put round the ears, and we all wore our black beret. The tank regiment was at that time the only regiment to wear a beret. Very thick leather gauntlets covered the hands, so that the whole body was then protected, and a sweat rag was put round the neck. On the left chest we carried three packs of chloroform pads, three hypodermic needles of morphia and three pep pills. The pep pills were of course to keep us going long after we would have collapsed with exhaustion. The morphia was for attending other members of the crew if wounded and in pain, or if they had cracked mentally and had to be quietened down. The orders were that if any of these things were used, the invalid was to be taken out of the tank and left wherever we were at the time, hopefully to be found by the first aid parties.

When getting into the tank, each member of the crew connected himself to a snatch plug which provided intercommunication with each other, incoming and outgoing radio messages, and gave the commander telephone communication with the infantry. Each tank carried five transmitters and receivers. The driver and the co-driver sat side by side at the front of the tank. The driver had instruments to his front and to his right, also a compass and a compass binnacle, which enabled us to travel on compass lines if necessary. When in action the driver used a periscope to see where he was going. The co-driver had a Besa machine gun with telescopic sights, and also used a periscope. To his left was a food bin, in which our rations were stored. These consisted mainly of dehydrated foodstuffs, owing to the shortage of space to store anything. The turret crew had even less room to move.

When looking at a tank, you can see the main gun, and what length is outside must be balanced with the same mass inside, and when fired it recoils two and a half feet. There was no room for safety shields so the operator and the commander had always to be vigilant, and not get in the way of the recoil. The gunner sat on an adjustable seat, right hand on the triggers, and left hand on the traverse handle. He had a periscope and also a telescope. The periscope had a view of the outside, but the telescope was his main instrument, as this gave him a very enlarged view of the target. The operator's job was to generally manage the transmitters and receivers, and the telephone, which kept the infantry in touch with the crew, when they used a handset from outside on the back of the tank. Also one of his main duties was to keep both turret guns loaded at all times. He also operated the grenade throwers, smoke bombs, parachute flares, signal flares etc. and made sure that they were ready at all times, to dispatch with the aid of the gunner.

The commander, as the name implies, commands the tank and crew, although he was not necessarily a commander in rank. He operated using a revolving cupola with six periscopes, he was in direct contact with the regimental command, the squadron command, the other tanks in the troop, the infantry command, the local infantry commander and of course the tank crew. Unlike the RAF crews who had ground staff to do all the cleaning and loading for them, the five men of the tank crew mucked in to do all their own cleaning and see to their own supplies, and loading etc.

The Churchill Tank was 42 tons in weight, it had a petrol engine, which on good roads and in good conditions would do four miles to the gallon, but in heavy going over muddy fields it would do four gallons to the mile. As far as I remember we carried about 120 gallons of petrol. It had a crash gearbox and differential steering, which meant it could turn round in its own length, by one track going forward and the other track going backwards. During any action, the bulkhead between the fighting compartment and the engine compartment would be left open so that the fans which cooled the engine would drag the air right through the tank to convey a lot of the fumes outside. It meant that there was a terrific noise from the engine all the time, but at least we could operate without being choked by all the different fumes. We could emit smoke from the rear, in the same way that a naval ship does from its funnel. It meant that one tank would be told to run across the front of any action emitting smoke to shield the rest of the squadron, and hide what action they were taking. It was taught and generally accepted that after penetration of the tank by an armour piercing shell, one only had about 4 to 5 seconds to bail out.

* * *

CHAPTER SIX

North Africa

It was now 1943, and we were in Tunisia. It was during our first few months in Africa that we worked with the Australian Infantry. They were good to work with. One thing that has stuck in my mind is a song that they often sang at night. I think for sentimental reasons, but of course they would never agree with that. The song went like this: -

In a lone Australian homestead
With the roses round the door,
A girl received a letter
Which had come right from the war.
With her mother's arms around her
She gave way to sobs and sighs,
And as she read that letter,
Then the tears came from her eyes.
Why should I weep, why should I cry,
My love's asleep so far away.
He gave his life that glorious day,
He gave his life for Suvla Bay.

It was very moving listening to songs like this during the quiet African nights. These men, almost uncivilised by the killings and hardships of war, yet they would sing this type of song with such feeling.

In 1982 and in later years, Maureen and I have visited Australia always asking about this Australian song, but no one knew it. Then on our fifth trip down under, we visited a small railway station near Toowoomba, and we arrived just as some Australian ex-servicemen were finishing their annual re-union, and they were singing that song. I talked to a couple of the men who explained that the song was from the 1914-1918 war, about the Dardenelles, and it made my day.

Also about the same time, we could hear the Germans singing. They also sang their songs with much feeling, especially *Lili Marlene*. I was surprised when our own people started singing the same song later, but in a jazzed up way. It was not nearly as nice as the German's version.

Christmas and New Year were just ordinary days to us. One small incident I remember stuck in my mind, maybe because it happened to a Lancashire man. We were advancing over flat open country when over the radio orders came to halt. Only a few yards away from us was a crack in the ground or a small wadi, so we straddled this with the tank, and being true English men, some of us got under the tank and boiled some water to make tea. It became obvious to us that this wadi was being used for the walking wounded, and prisoners of war, to get to the rear safely. We were drinking our tea, when a British soldier came round the bend going to the rear to the first aid post. We could see that he had a jagged sliver of steel about fifteen inches long through his face. It had gone in one cheek near his mouth and out the other. Behind him were two Italian soldiers, and behind them a very large German soldier. When the Lancashire Fusilier soldier came up to us, we told him to sit on the side for a rest, and he gratefully sat down. When the Italians come up to him, they saw he was helpless and they spat on him. The German soldier behind them became enraged when he saw this, and grabbed both Italians by their necks and smashed their heads together. He then threw them on one side, both unconscious, and picked up the Lancashire Fusilier like a baby and carried on down to the first aid post. When we continued our advance, we left the two Italians still unconscious in the ditch.

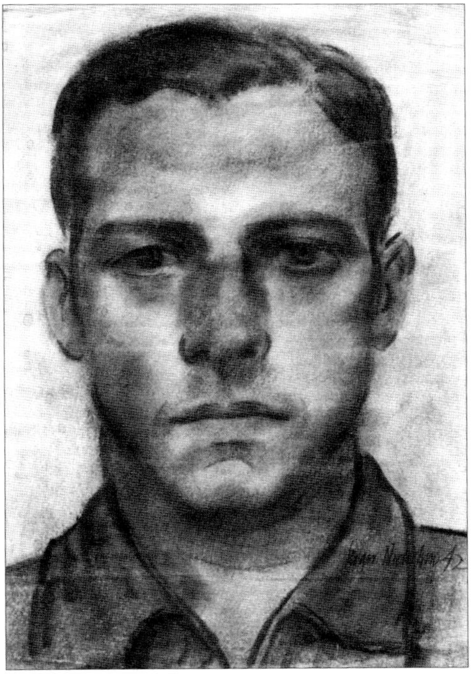

Pastel drawing by my friend Roger Nicolson, Tunisia 1943

By this time our personal hygiene and comfort was getting from bad to worse. The heat in the tank was unbearable. The steel of the tank heated up during the day, and did not cool much at night, so heated up even more each succeeding day. If any of us touched the inside of the tank with our bare flesh, it would blister. We were all suffering from a sweat rash, mainly under the arms and the chest, in the crotch and the inside of the legs. Some of the sweat rashes were so bad they were bleeding, and were very painful. We had asked base to send us some cream or something, but nothing ever arrived. To add to our discomfort, the water container in the tank only held two and a half gallons, which was only half a gallon per man per day. This was not enough to drink in a day, let alone have a wash or wash our underwear, and consequently our clothing rotted on us. We requested, clothing, creams, shaving tackle and soap, but nothing ever came up with our supplies. So eventually we all had beards, long hair, and all smelt rather rotten. We took to stopping at any house we came across looking for any clothes that might be there, and helping ourselves, if there were any trousers or shirts. We were not very lucky in this respect most times, as there was rarely anything left behind by the occupants, who had fled. We also looked for food, because as time went by this commodity got scarcer, and our supplies more infrequent. Everything had to travel from England out to us, via civilian transport, docks, ships, the Service Corps in both England and Tunisia, to Service HQ then Brigade HQ and on to our own supply echelons and lastly to the men in the line in the tanks, and by the time they reached us, there was hardly anything left. The Infantry suffered in the same way, as they were also last in the line for supply. Yet we were all the men in the front line and expected to do all the fighting in the state we were left in. We did find a pig one day, and I said I would kill it. I put my revolver to his head and fired six rounds, but he only grunted and carried on feeding. Then one of the others tied it to a tree and cut its throat. That night all the squadron had pork.

After forming a laager one night, we waited for our supplies but our supply echelon were late getting to us. By the time they did reach us it was dark, and after delivering essentials like fuel and ammunition, the sergeant major came up asking, "Where is Frank? I have a parcel for him, and I know it is for him even though I can't read the name in the dark, as this is the only one brought up to-day." This was the one and only parcel that I ever received during the duration of the war. After opening it in the dark, I felt a jar of what I thought was Vaseline. I rejoiced in this and taking off my trousers, I scooped a generous helping of the cream and rubbed it all over my rashes. What bliss I thought, but two minutes after I suffered, as it burnt like hell, and in the morning I found that it was Wintergreen ointment! All the others thought it a great joke.

*

It was about March 1943 when my squadron was advancing across a plain, I think it was called the Goubelat plain, when we came upon a dried up riverbed. We immediately realised that getting to the other side would be very dangerous because a rough concrete road had been laid some years previously. It was obvious to us that if the riverbed could not take civilian traffic, it certainly could not take the weight of the tanks. It was decided that the infantry would go to ground, while three tanks in line ahead, would attempt the crossing. The infantry had suffered many casualties when they had arrived at the dried up riverbed, and while waiting to decide what to do, they brought up a three ton truck to take the wounded away. The three tanks advanced with about a hundred yards between them, but when the lead tank was half way across an anti tank gun opened up from the other side and the lead tank exploded, killing all the crew.

The other two tanks started to reverse out of range, the crews keeping their eyes glued on the other side of the riverbed, trying to locate the German positions. However, the truck with the wounded infantrymen was on our side of the riverbed, and the tank reversing not knowing it was there, went over the truck killing most of the men in it. The two tanks got back safely, but it was a terrible calamity to happen. We did eventually get across the riverbed, after pounding the other side out of existence.

As explained before, the only storage inside the tank, was the food bin next to the co-driver, which is only about one and a half cubic feet in size (I think in feet not being in metric yet), and mostly everything else is carried bolted onto the outside of the tank. We each started with a metal bin, which was bolted to the outside of the turret, but they only lasted a short time. We started with a blanket each, some cooking things and some tin plates, and some personal things in these bins, but in no time at all they were shot to pieces. Anything we could lay our hands on was fastened with bits of wire or rope to the outside of the tank, these might at some time prove useful and they served to alter the outline of the tank. I found two things that proved very useful to us; one was an angle iron box arrangement the other was a lavatory seat! Whenever we camped or formed a laager, we would dig a hole put the angle iron arrangement over it and place the wooden toilet seat on top. We were the envy of the squadron, and the colonel and even the squadron commander would come and ask if they could use our toilet. Even General Crocker, came to use it, and I remember him clearly sitting there in full view of everyone and drinking tea while performing. He also would smoke his pipe such as it was, as he complained that he had broken the stem and it was so short now that he burnt his nose.

If we found any broken tank tracks, or our own had to be changed, we would have them welded onto the outside of the tank by the fitters, they provided us with extra armour. It was also a comfort to us, making us feel safer with the extra protection. When living in these conditions, men revert to becoming more like animals than humans, and we lived just for the moment not thinking of anything else. We were dirty, we were full of lice, did not have enough food or water, did not have any change of clothing, and we never got any leave. Occasionally we would have a five day or seven day rest period, but that time was spent repairing engines, and tracks and anything else that needed seeing to, which were numerous enough to keep us busy the whole time. It was during these rest periods that we would try to have a wash down using a canvas bucket, as we would get a little more water sent up then.

By this time we were coming in contact with the Americans, and we were not very happy about this. Most places in Africa have only one road, in not very good condition and not very wide. In the British Forces our main priorities for using the road were different to the Americans. We put ambulances, food, water, ammunition and fuel as priorities, but the Americans did no such thing, and would crowd the roads with their laundry vehicles and even ice cream vans, as they were unable to survive without their ice cream! This could be fatal because of the difficulty of getting the wounded to the rear, to the first aid or the forward hospital.

They had vast quantities of food, but although we were down to half a tin of bully and four army biscuits a day, they would destroy their stores by setting fire to it rather than give it to us, unless we would give them a German Luger pistol or an Italian Berretta pistol. We found out that these were then sent to their homes with stories of how they had won them in fights against the Germans and Italians. We were not allowed to send anything home, so they were useless to us anyway. During this period we all lost a lot of weight. Not only through shortage of food but also from the heat inside the tanks. I went down to about seven and a half stones.

I smile when I hear about newspaper correspondents being at the front, and reporting what is happening. Not one of us had ever seen any of them. Also singers and entertainers, who were supposed to have entertained the troops in the front line, never went nearer than the rear headquarters. We did once come across some cameramen. We were on a plain, overlooked by a twin peaked mountain, nicknamed by us crude soldiers as Queen Sheba's Tits. The correct name being, "*Jebel bou Kornine*". Both these peaks were occupied by German lookouts. All the squadron were arranged in full view but out of range of these lookouts, to act as decoy for the German guns and armour, so as to keep them occupied whilst the other British troops were assembling to make an attack some twenty miles away. We stayed there for ten days and nights. Because of the heat and flies during the day we all contracted dysentery, which brought more flies. As we were all forced to relieve ourselves, the only place to do this inside a tank is through a dump hole beside the co-drivers seat. The real purpose of this hole is to get rid of empty shell cases whenever possible. The space is only about three feet high and the hole only about five inches wide, so you can imagine how difficult things were.

It was during this waiting time that I had my 21st Birthday! For my treat the crew let me have a spoonful of sugar in my tea, and that is all I ever got for my 21st.

Each day at a pre-arranged signal each tank took it in turns to go to the rear, about three quarters of a mile to a little quarry where every day a water truck came, and every third day a petrol and a food truck were there. We followed the same procedure each time it was our turn, and on my Birthday it was the same. As we were all suffering from dysentery and we only had a short time in which to do everything, we all got undressed before arriving at the quarry. We turned into the quarry at speed and then slammed on the breaks, making a huge cloud of dust.

We all jumped out and squatted outside the tank with no trousers on, so that we were able to relieve ourselves quickly. As the cloud of dust began to settle we got the shock of our lives, because about twenty yards in front of us there was a party of newspaper and newsreel cameramen with their cameras rolling. They cursed us when they saw what we were doing, as they had wanted to film the victorious soldiers arriving from the battlefront to show the people at home, and all they got were five bare bottoms doing what comes naturally. I wonder if this newsreel is in the archives somewhere, and will it get shown sometime on “Glorious Muck Ups”?

Each tank was allowed only half an hour then it was back to the front again until the next day. Two or three days later we again turned into the quarry, we all climbed out and I was carrying a little petrol stove that we used to brew our tea on. I carried it to a little trench to put it in to light it, as it was a bit breezy that day. As

I jumped in I thought I heard someone call me, but there was no-one there, then I looked down and where the breeze had blown the sand away, I saw a dead German in the trench. I had jumped on his stomach, and the air pressed out of his lungs had made the noise. Believe me I jumped out of there in double quick time.

Occasionally when on a rest period, the delousing van would call on us. All the squadron would gather round and each of us in turn would get a wire tray from the van, then strip off and put all our clothing in the tray and anything else that might be infected. We would then sit around for an hour while all our belongings were subjected to killer fumes in the van. We would all feel a lot better after our treatment from what we called, "The Lousy Van". Another visitor we occasionally had was the dentist. He would arrive in his 15 cwt truck, sort his equipment out, and we would sit around on the ground waiting. His equipment consisted of a table with a tin of water on it, a drilling machine, which was powered by one leg operating a treadle, and an old dining chair for the patient to sit on. You can imagine waiting and watching the unfortunate person before you, being subjected to the treatment, knowing it was your turn next. There was the dentist standing on one leg and pumping the drill with the other, to treat an awkwardly positioned tooth.

Another strange thing happened. An Arab who must have left his own land because of the war passing, had returned, and to make sure that his land was safe, he tethered his donkeys to be looked after by his two sons, and then lined up his women. Presumably these were his wives and daughters. He then whipped them forward making them stamp their feet to ensure that there were no mines left behind. We watched as they went up and down, the women terrified in case they did step on a mine. It took about two hours before he was satisfied that the land was clear, and it was obvious to us who and what he valued most, it certainly was not the women.

It was plain to see that operations here were coming to an end. General Montgomery who was hated by every one of us, sent word that if Tunis was taken by a certain date everyone would have home leave. Tunis was taken and the African War had finished before the set date, but not one of us had any leave. The only person to get home leave was Montgomery himself and he left word that all wine shops and brothels were out of bounds, and everyone had to have physical training in the warmest part of the day.

After being in Africa for a short time, and having worked with numerous Regiments from different countries, we began to understand how various people worked and behaved. We liked working with the Australians and New Zealanders, and also the South Africans.

The squadron was going through a pass in the Atlas Mountains when orders came over the radio to pull off the road for one hour. We did the usual; made some tea and had something to eat.

The first time we worked with the Foreign Legion they were very pleased to be with a Tank Regiment, as they had not worked with tanks before. They were very happy as they had not lost any men and everything went smoothly.

The Commanding Officer of the Legion said he wanted to award every man in the Regiment with the Croix de Guerre. Our Commanding Officer refused this however, and said he would accept only five. He received one himself, the second in command had one, and the other three we had to draw cards for by the rest of us. One was drawn by an Officer, one by the Sergeant Major who never got into any action, and one by a member of one of the tank crews.

It makes one wonder if there was any value on any of the medals won, or was it just a lottery. I have never worn any of my medals, as I consider them valueless.

One evening we were all very busy doing essential jobs in preparation for the next day.

One of the crews was refuelling, putting petrol in their tank from jerry cans, and probably spilling a little.

What they had not noticed was that the tank had become so hot that it was vaporising the petrol and the fumes were slowly moving along the ground towards some Senegalese troops who had a fire nearby. When the fumes reached the fire it acted like a fuse and flashed back to the tank exploding the jerry can being emptied. Fortunately it blew the crew off of the tank, then the petrol tanks inside the tank exploded. This reached the ammunition and this exploded completely wrecking the tank.

Another similar thing happened to another tank when the operator was loading ammunition in his tank. He had finished loading the hull and had started loading the ready use racks. These were on the turret floor in a very convenient position for use when in action. The commander was standing on the outside of the turret handing the shells down through the hatchway to the operator. Some of these shells were armour piercing and some were high explosives.

We think he may have loaded the high explosive shells, and then when loading the armour piercing shells he let one slip and it must have pierced one of the high explosive shells, starting the mechanism and starting the reaction, and then all the ammunition in the tank blew up. The commander was blown clear thank heaven, but the operator who was inside caught the full blast and was killed.

My Regiment who were camped on the outskirts of Tunis, were told to prepare for the victory parade, and for some unknown reason my tank "Ardent" was chosen to be on the right of the saluting base. On the big day of the Victory March we borrowed khaki drill uniforms from our back echelons which still had theirs, as our were in tatters. The tank was cleaned up and manoeuvred into its prime position next to the saluting base. The remainder of the squadron lined up facing the saluting base. While we were waiting for the march past to begin, a young French lady came from the crowd and asked me why a British Tank had a French name, and I explained to her that "Ardent" meant the same in English as it did in French, and she told me that it was her father who was curious. After she had gone the march started and the military bands played, and it was certainly a day to remember. After the parade had finished, back came the young French lady with her father beside her. We were introduced; his name was Mons. Guillard, and my friend and I were invited to go to their home for dinner. Roger Nicholson and I duly arrived at their house, and during the conversation he told us he was the head archaeologist for the whole of Tunisia, his daughter's name was Suzanne, she was the English teacher at the High School. It was a bungalow type of house with a flat roof they used for dancing and parties, the dinner was out of this world, I had never experienced anything like it before. There were eight courses with a different wine for each course and we finished with chocolate and brandy. The party consisted of Mons.& Mme. Guillard, Suzanne, together with two of her friends, Lillian and Denise, and of course Roger and myself. Roger was normally known as Nick, an abbreviation of his surname, but when I introduced him as Nick the entire party looked embarrassed and blushed. We found out later that the word "nick" was a rude word in Tunisia and from then on he was to be known as Roger.

* * *

CHAPTER SEVEN

Isolated and forgotten

From Tunis we were moved about twenty-five miles to an isolated area called Ainmokra. Supposedly for rest and recuperation, but with heavy tanks we were not welcome in civilised areas. It was a completely wild area with a little Arab village about three miles away. Here we went into communal catering, everyone helping to make a kitchen out of palm trees. We still had no tents or toilets, or any plates or mugs, or anything to wear. If it rained, everyone walked around naked to save getting what we did have getting wet. Each day a truck would go to headquarters for supplies, and our crew asked the truck drivers to call at a small shop near headquarters where they could buy a barrel of very crude jungle juice wine. When they returned the barrel would be placed on a rock or mound of earth and we would sit around it continually filling our tins (which were opened bean tins with the lid turned back for a handle not having any mugs), all the crews would do the same, until one by one each man would fall back unconscious. It seems a very stupid thing to do, but by then, we had lost any civilised behaviour, and had reverted to being almost like animals again. The Infantry were the same, and we often compared the life of an infantryman and tank crew with the life of a RAF crew. The RAF had ground staff for servicing their planes, loading, re-fuelling and cleaning etc., they had beds with sheets on to sleep in at night, bar rooms and canteens, double rations of food, regular leave, and could go out at night to meet their girl friends. Pubs were available and they had much better pay. We were very envious.

The Colonel decided we must have a canteen, so he applied to the Naafi but they refused to come out, he had the same reply from TOC H, Church of England, Church of Scotland, and the Catholic Church canteens, none would come out to our deserted spot. As a last resort he asked the Salvation Army, and to his joy they answered, "Yes". They enquired where we were and how to get there, and said they would be with us in three days. On the third day, as promised, a 3 cwt truck came bouncing up the track, and two middle aged ladies got out. They must have had the shock of their lives, for we still had nothing, not even a piece of sacking to put round the toilet. They produced two tents, one for living in and one for storage, and also a canvas toilet. We erected the tents for them and made a clay oven as instructed. Two days later, these two stalwart ladies announced that they would open the next day at 6.0 pm.

They only had a table in front of the tent on which to put the rock buns they had made, and the urns of tea. The opening time arrived, and we all lined up. What a sight we were, we all had long hair and beards, some with boots on and some bare footed, all had shorts or cut down trousers, and we all had our tins. Poor ladies, we must have been the roughest looking men they had ever seen. However, one of them called for silence, and said that before they served the tea and rock buns, we would all sing a song, which was "Jesus wants me for a Sunbeam"!!! She beat out the time, and the singing started but the language was atrocious! She stopped us, and it was only after persevering that on the sixth attempt she managed to get us singing the correct words. Having achieved this, they then served us all with our tea and rock bun, and we were truly grateful for this treat. They were two really wonderful ladies, and were loved and respected by everyone.

There was still no sign of tents coming our way so we looked around the area and found that about two miles away there was a railway line. Part of it was very steep and the steam engines had a hard time pulling up the steep gradient. This was our opportunity, and over a period of about two weeks in the evenings we hid in the trees and when the train went past slowly up the incline, we jumped on board and stole the ropes and sheets of tarpaulin from the rearmost wagons. They were quite heavy to carry back to the camp, but we did manage it, and with these sheets of tarpaulin and rope, and some trees that we chopped down, we made a number of huts. Each one could hold about fourteen men. Holes were cut out for doors and windows, and a piece of tarpaulin was made to let down in the doorway at night. Also we made camp beds, and these were quite a luxury after sleeping on the floor for so long.

It was surprising that from that time on our spirits surged upwards and life became almost normal. Also at this time we began to receive uniforms and other necessities, and we started to become human again. We still looked like a load of tramps though, and the commanding officer must have thought so too. He got in touch with the commanding officer of a Guards Regiment, about fifteen miles away and consequently a Drill Sergeant Major came to our squadron to smarten us up. A dozen of us non-commissioned officers were on parade the first day, he marched us up and down a few times, and swore at me telling me that I was swaying about like a bloody galleon on a rough sea! One by one we had to march the squadron backwards and forwards, and when it was my turn I had to march them away from me. However when they were about two hundred yards away I was told to about turn them, I screamed my head off but no one could hear me. The Drill Sergeant Major seemed to quietly say about turn, and back they came. He said we were all bloody hopeless, and went back to his regiment, and we all said thank goodness for that.

One day four of us decided to have a walk to see what the Arab village was like. It was only a short distance away, but as usual when leaving the camp we were all armed with revolvers. At this village the buildings consisted of mainly mud huts, around a sort of village green, but with no grass. It was a depressing place.

Now that we were respectable with new uniforms, clean hands and faces, and polished boots, we were allowed half a day each week in the nearest town, which was called Bone on the Algerian coast. It was about thirty-five miles away, and a truck was laid on each day at noon to take us there and returned from Bone at 5.0pm. It was a miserable little town, with a few cafes selling cheap wines, and a few Arabs selling filthy postcards. Nick and I usually found a fairly clean café where we talked to men of other Regiments and sometimes with seamen.

It was the meeting of a Naval Captain in a café that lead to Nick and I being invited to go minesweeping in the Mediterranean, for two weeks. The minesweeper was a converted trawler called *Fluelyn*. After getting permission from our Commanding Officer we set sail, sweeping towards the island of Sicily, turning back when in sight of the coast, and then sweeping back towards Bone. We never found any mines, but we thoroughly enjoyed the change.

It was in a café in Bone that we heard of how American Dakotas carrying three hundred British airborne troops to Sicily, had panicked when two German Messerschmidts came near them, and had dropped them well short of the target, all the men being drowned in the Mediterranean. It was never reported in the papers presumably because it would have left bad feelings between the Allies.

We were also occasionally able to arrange a trip to Tunis, where we again visited Mons. & Mme. Guillard, their daughter Susan and her two friends. It was during our last visit there that Mons. Guillard gave me a present of a few coins, which had been found in Carthage. Susan gave me a hand carved silver scorpion on a silver chain, both were over three thousand years old, she put the chain and scorpion round my neck, saying that it would keep me safe. Unfortunately later in Italy when I was under anaesthetic someone took it from me, probably not realising its value and I never got it back.

Mons. Guillard wanted me to marry Susan. If I wanted to come back after the war was over he was in a position to help me to return there by legally adopting me to get admission into Tunis, then disowning me, leaving me free to marry Susan. However it never came to pass, as I never got the opportunity to return, and life went on elsewhere.

Back at the camp some of the men had made a shower from a fifty-gallon drum, raised about twelve feet in the air with a steel plate under it where a fire could be lit to heat the water. Water was pumped up to it from the water tanker, and once the fire was lit and the water warm, the tap was turned on letting the water run through two pipes which had holes in them, letting the water down onto the men waiting under the pipes. We had to be very quick to swill off before all the water ran out.

During our period of waiting between the end of the African Campaign and the start of the Italian Campaign, we managed a trip to Constantine in Algeria. This was a strange city split down the middle by a crack in the rock. Apart from the crack there was nothing of note. What brings this city to mind is that while walking around we came upon a little girl being whipped by her brother who was about a year older than her. When we tried to stop him, a Catholic Priest came to us and asked that we did not stop him, saying that if we did the boy would tell his father and then he would whip her ten times harder to teach her that she must submit to her brother. What a hard life some of these girls and women lived.

My friend Nick who was an artist, asked me to sit with him while he painted a scene, and this surprised me until we arrived at the scene he wanted to paint. This was a native brothel in Bone! We were there for about four hours, and when he had finished he put it with his other paintings and they were sent to the War Museum in London, where they were accepted, and as far as I know they are still there as official record.

* * *

CHAPTER EIGHT

Promotion and Italian campaign

It was about this time that there was a big sort out of personnel, and I was made war substantive, and commander of the tank "Apollo". The second commander was David Owen, he took over "Ajax", and the third commander was Jim Bunting who took "Achilles". As we all got on very well together, it was a most desirable position to be in, as each mans life depended on every other member of the troop. There was also a draft intake of new recruits from England, to fill the vacancies, and I selected one as the co-driver, named Tommy (I am at the moment unable to recall his second name). We realised that with all these events taking place, something was in the offing. The next thing was a complete medical for everyone, and we all passed A.1. Here I must confess that I have never been A.1 because my left eye has always been much weaker than my right one. Twice before when having a medical in the offing, I had broken into the medical room the night before and copied the eye chart to memorise. This time was no exception, and as the room was only a tent, I managed to get in during the middle of the night without being seen, by loosening the tent walls and slipping inside. I made my usual copy of the chart and returned to my quarters to memorise it. The next day I passed A.1. I considered it my duty to stay with the fighting part of the squadron, in the tank crews, as basically I thought that every man should fight for his country if he is capable and fit enough.

A week later I developed a sore throat so the medical officer decided to send me to an army hospital. This was the usual tented hospital, and I was there for about two weeks. During this time some of the wounded from Southern Italy were brought in. Many were very bad cases, but the worst of all were the Mustard Gas victims. They were terrible to look at and all eventually died. They had been on the docks in the South Italian city of Bari, where a ship loaded with the Mustard Gas had exploded, when bombed by the Germans. It was shortly after this that I was very relieved to return to my unit.

One afternoon we were called together and given four hours notice to move. The tanks were already fully loaded and in perfect order, and two hours later the tank transporters arrived. We were then loaded onto them; by this time it was dark and we moved off. We arrived at a beach not far from Bone, in Algeria, and there waiting for us were the LSTs in army terms, landing ship tanks. We reversed on; three tanks per ship and set sail for Italy. The ships were beached near Salerno; we rolled off immediately and proceeded to a wood a little further inland, where we stayed until dark. There was enough time for a rest, a meal and to get the tanks into service condition, just in case we met anything on the road. When darkness came we moved north in column, driving only with ultra violet lights, stopping every two hours for a check over. We rested during the day, once again out of sight, and then completed our journey the following night.

We arrived at a little town near Naples called Caserta and parked under the walls of the Victor Emmanuel's Palace. Where we stopped there was a hole in the wall, presumably made by a shell hitting it, so we dug our lavatory hole in the gardens and proudly put our lavatory seat over it. This was a rest period, and as there was very little needed doing to the tanks; it really was a rest period.

One day four of us borrowed a Jeep without permission and

took a trip to Pompeii, we were most impressed with the ancient town, which we had not realised was so big. On returning we passed through Naples just to see what it was like. It was while we were here that Vesuvius erupted spreading ash for miles around. The population of Naples were having a very bad time, as there was no food of any sort to be had anywhere. The British Army was issuing hard tack biscuits where they could, and even babies had to survive on these, after first being chewed by their mothers to soften them, and then being spit into their mouths.

About a hundred yards from our tank was a barber's shop, and we decided it was about time we had a hair cut. He also sold wine and cheap Champagne, so we also had some of this. His daughter was in the next room offering her services to anyone who could pay, and two of our men disappeared for a short time!! It was a way of thinking to some of us, that if you caught VD you would have to be hospitalised for four months, and that meant you were guaranteed another four months to live, which could not be guaranteed when living with the tank crews.

We thoroughly enjoyed our rest, although of course every member of the crew was still doing his share of night guard duty. This had been continued every day since we landed in Africa, and none of us had had a full nights sleep since then. The rest period was over, and that night we moved north towards Cassino. When about five miles from Cassino, everywhere had turned to mud. We found out afterwards that the Germans had breeched the Rapido River and flooded the whole countryside around the town. Our squadron moved to about two miles from Cassino, then waited for three days on full alert. No supplies of any description could be brought up by truck, because of the mud, so a regiment of South African Basuto brought everything up on the backs of mules, including petrol and oil. During this hellish three days, we could see the continuous shelling of Cassino town and the Monastery on top of the mountain. During these three days, over a thousand bombers dropped their full loads of bombs on the Monastery each day in an attempt to soften up the opposition. We found out later that it was a complete waste of time.

On the evening of the third day the Canadian Infantry joined us, we chatted and grumbled together, as soldiers normally do, until about three o'clock in the morning, orders were received that we were to move forward, carrying the Canadian Infantry, because of the atrocious conditions. We moved to our starter positions and at dawn the squadron commander broke radio silence with "Squadron Advance". Unlike some forces who say "Tally Ho", I said to my crew in crude army speak, "Shit or Bust lads, advance". We engaged enemy tanks, guns and men, and then all hell was let loose. There were explosions all around us, smoke and dust cut down our vision and great mounds of earth were thrown up and over us. I had never experienced such density of opposition in all my life before. Everything happened so fast that my mind could not take it all in, and I do not remember it in detail, until at last we became stationary, for no obvious cause. The engine was still roaring away, and on the intercom I asked my driver if something was wrong, but he said that there was nothing wrong, the engine was still engaging, the tracks were still going round but we were not moving. Then looking through the cupola periscopes I saw that for some reason another tank had climbed on top of us, very effectively bring us to a halt. The only thing to do was to get out and investigate. I just managed to squeeze through the open cupola; dropped to the ground and made my way round to the rear of the other tank. I got there just as four of the crew bailed out, and they told me that their commander was dead, and they were going back to HQ, so off they went. I looked in the tank hoping they had made a mistake, but they had not, and the commander, Ronny Langley, who had been a personal friend of mine, had for some unknown reason, put his head out of the hatch and it had been blown off. The attack had by this time moved on a little, so for safety I ordered my crew to switch off and bail out as well. We all congregated under the other tank, as there were still a lot of missiles flying about us, and it was then that I noticed my new co-driver was in a bad way. His nerve had gone. By this time quite of a lot of German prisoners were making their way to the rear to the prisoners compound, and I called three of them over to ask them to take my co-driver back to the First Aid post, which they did willingly. A little later I sent another three members of my crew back to HQ and they had not been gone long when David Owen my troop leader came over. He had also lost his tank and was making his way back, but on seeing me with these two tanks, came over and we discussed the situation. We decided that in case the Germans put in a counter attack we could not possibly leave these two tanks for them to use. So I climbed in the driver's position of Ronny's tank, and David climbed into mine. By jerking the clutch violently we managed to separate them, but then I could not get mine to start. So we hitched them together with one of the steel towropes, and David started to tow me towards our HQ in a very low gear. We came to a raised hedge, and David went over still towing me, but when I came to it I went over the raised part and it slammed down the other side. This made the dead body in the other compartment fly over me hitting me in the head and shoulder. Some liquid spurted out of his lungs over my head and chest, which made me feel quite sick.

We eventually got back to HQ and I dismounted feeling a little rough, the build up of what had happened over the last few days and what had just occurred had taken its toll. So I grabbed a blanket and rolled under the tank to have a rest. David had reported to H.Q. and in few minutes he came back saying that he had volunteered himself, with me and three others, to try and penetrate the German lines to link up with the Princess Patricia's Canadian light infantry, who were completely surrounded. We mounted the tank with me as driver and waited for permission to move off. After a short period of waiting, the colonel came over and told us to dismount, as there was no point in us going, because the entire regiment had been wiped out. I think that this action by David in making me get into the tank again for action made me pull myself together and I was nearly myself again. We were relieved that we had not had to go in, but at the same time we were very sorry that we were unable to help them.

It was on this day that as one of our tanks advanced he came to a small clearing with a large tree in the middle, under this tree were about a hundred wounded men, Germans, Canadian and British, with three German Red Cross men looking after them. These Red Cross workers asked that our colonel be sent a request for medical supplies as theirs had run out. This was done, supplies were sent to them and the colonel went down to see what was happening for himself. On arriving and seeing what was happening at first hand, he detailed one of his men to take the three Red Cross men back to their own lines then he shook their hands and off they went.

It was after my regiment and the Canadian first division broke what was called the Gustav line at Cassino that I believe the fourth and tenth armoured divisions went through to keep the Germans on the move.

I did hear that we lost thirty-seven tanks that day.

* * *

CHAPTER NINE

Coriano Ridge

It was now September 1944 and we were near the little Italian town of Coriano, just a few miles south east of San Morino and on a ridge running east to west. We had teamed up with the Scottish Regiment, The Argylles, to attack north at dawn the following day. Well before dawn the squadron together with the infantry moved onto the area known as the Coriano ridge, taking up a hull down position. This means that the tanks are not visible to the enemy, but the tank commanders from the height of their turrets can see over to the position taken up by the enemy. We were to advance line abreast, and as normal there was to be complete radio silence. The objective was the next line of hills a few miles ahead. As dawn broke and the sky became lighter, at the prearranged time, radio silence was broken by the order to advance. We started with our usual saying, "Here we go again, shit or bust, driver advance".

I remember very clearly that as we went over the ridge, the tune *Nimrod* by Elgar was going through my head, and as I swung the cupola to the left and right, I could see the whole squadron of our heavy tanks advancing. I thought what a powerful sight they made, and now whenever I hear the tune of *Nimrod* I remember that morning. We carried on at infantry pace then to my right, one tank simply vanished. He was going over a pile of rubble, which was probably a wrecked farmhouse, and the floor gave way under him with the weight of the tank, and deposited him in the

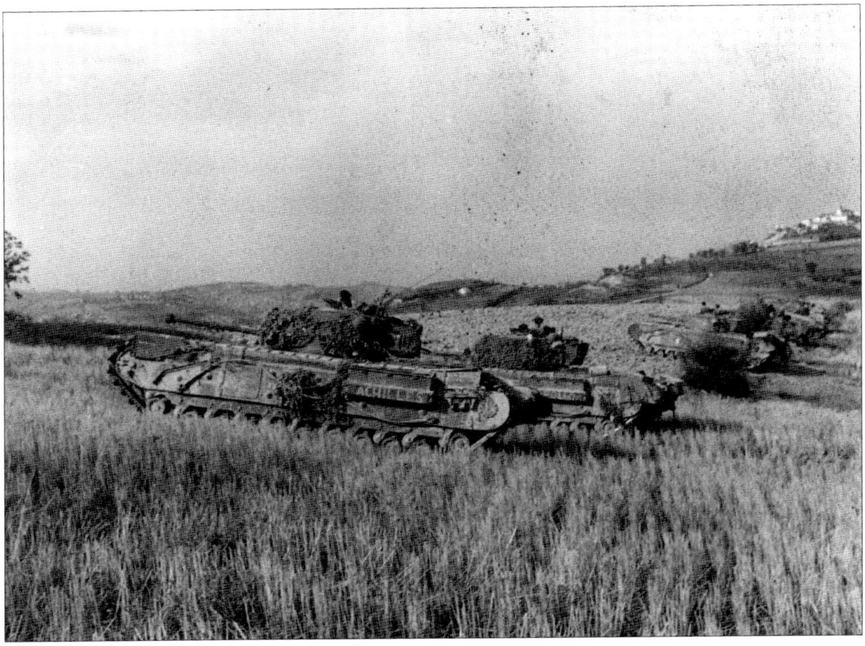

My Apollo tank second from left © Imperial War Museum

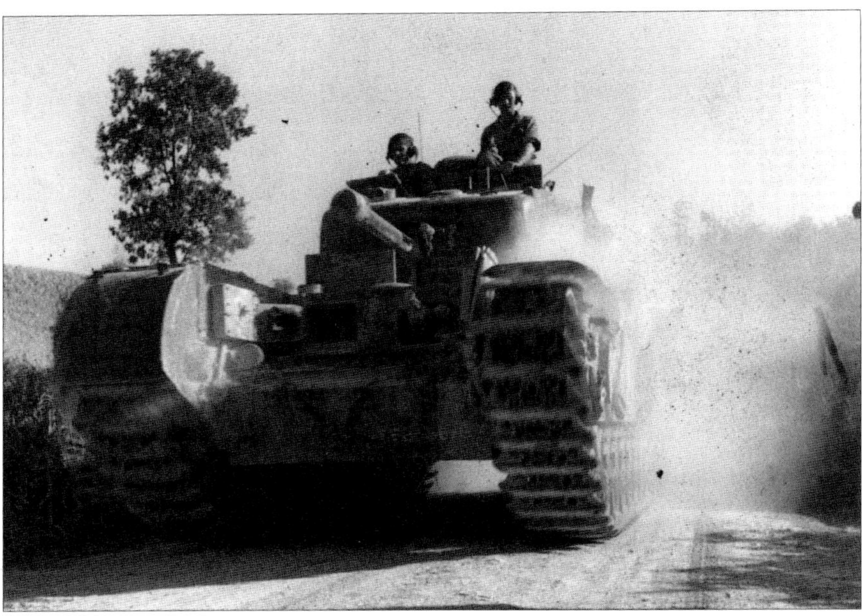

Driver identified as Arthur Egerton © Imperial War Museum

cellars, from which he could not get out. The squadron continued advancing across a stream, and then things began getting really rough. From then on we were occupied with looking after ourselves and reaching our objective. The Argylles were having a hellish time and they went to ground and stayed there for the rest of the day. We received a fair amount of damage but I think we caused more damage than we received. With it being so hectic we lost all track of time, and it took me a while to realise that David Owen's tank and my tank were the only ones left out of the squadron.

The others one by one for different reasons had been knocked out. By this time we were moving slowly uphill towards our objective, and were in a very unenviable and vulnerable position. David suddenly called out to me on the radio "Watch out Frank there are Tiger tanks ahead". Just then a Tiger fired a shot at me but it hit the ground about three yards ahead of us. I had noticed a haystack to our left, and I quickly told the driver to advance left behind this. Immediately after the first shot had missed me, another shot hit David's tank on the front of the turret, penetrating and killing David, and he dropped on top of the gunner. I found all this out later. I saw the driver and co-driver bale out then Tommy Halsy, David's operator, pushed his flaps up to bale out but a shot from one of the Tigers hit the front flap and took half his face and his head off. I realised then that my tank Apollo was the only tank left out of the squadron of eighteen tanks, and I also knew that we did not stand a chance against whatever number of Tigers were waiting for us on top of the ridge. So I made a decision to attempt to go back, and just then I glanced back at David's tank and saw his head and shoulders coming up out of the cupola. I knew then that he must be dead, because what was happening was that the gunner with super human strength was pushing David's body up out of the tank where he had fallen on top of him so that he could bale out, and the last I saw of the gunner was him vanishing under a hedge.

While this was happening I had been trying to hide both our tanks by throwing out a smoke screen, but there was a lively breeze that day, and the smoke was quickly blown away. I ordered the driver to advance right and make full speed, and as we quickly made our way back to our own lines, we found ourselves being chased by two Spitfires who had been supporting us. Unfortunately for us, they saw a tank going the wrong way and thought the Germans were counter attacking, so they both attacked us, and I found out later that they had also radioed Divisional Headquarters and a full division of artillery was ordered to blast the area. So there we were on our own being strafed by two Spitfires and blasted by a full division of artillery. How we came out of it alive I have no idea, either our guardian angels were looking after us, or the gunners were rotten shots. However, they soon realised their mistake and the bombardment stopped.

When we were some distance from the Tiger tanks, I radioed headquarters and quickly explained what was happening. I was promptly ordered to turn round and make my way forward again, this time through the wood to my right, to take up a position at the northern most point, observe what was happening, and report back. I made my way to the edge of the wood and very slowly moved forward to a good observation point. Unfortunately they saw me first, and their first shot blew my right track off. I quickly ordered, "Bale out" and everyone baled out except Frank Cook my turret gunner. For some reason he did not bale out, and the next shot from the Tigers penetrated the turret ring area and killed him. The same shot hit the hydraulic brakes, and the tank rolled forward down the hill. Just to our rear there was an Italian farmhouse, and we made our way to this, going down into the cellar out of harms way. The cellar was full of the Italians, and we joined them sitting against the wall to wait. During that night a baby was born to one of the Italian women.

In the morning we went out and made our way towards our tank, there was no sign of any Germans about, and as we were extremely hungry, we thought we could get some of our food rations from the tank. We saw no signs of the enemy and thought they must have pulled out during the night. Not thinking, I climbed onto the tank pulled open the cupola flaps and was immediately covered with about ten thousand blue bottle flies. They poured out of the hatchway and stuck on my face. They must have been feeding on Frank during the night. I was terrified, and slamming the hatches closed; I beat a hasty retreat, all hunger forgotten. We eventually found our way back to our Headquarters.

On arrival at HQ we had the usual de-briefing and a meal. Our HQ was really only three tanks, two armoured cars, a radio truck and a few jeeps. Then we found the remainder of A Squadron and found that most of the tanks had been lost and quite a number of the men. I cannot remember exactly how many but in my troop there were five dead, including David Owen who had undoubtedly saved my life that day. It took only a week to replace the tanks and the men, then we moved two or three miles to the east, where the line was at a stand still. When we arrived at the rendezvous area, we found the Argylles waiting for us and another big push was organised for the following day. This push again commenced on the Coriano Ridge, but a little further east. Once again it was very heavy going, and more tanks and men were lost.

By way of explanation, when the Navy and Air force are winning they decimate the opposition making it easier to further decimate them, when the Army is winning it means they are advancing and it is in the open and can be seen by the enemy. The hidden enemy from their positions can defend themselves in many ways. Mines for instance. So troops advancing always have more casualties of men and machines than the defenders.

Back to the day in question, it soon became too heavy for the Argylles; they were pinned down unable to move. The remainder of us carried on and eventually I became aware that I was the only tank in sight, we were about a mile forward of the infantry and the only tanks I could see were a few behind us which were on fire. A few minutes later something hit us on one of the front sprockets, and although we tried to go forward, with the damaged sprocket the track came off, putting us out of action. Once again we were in the open and unable to move. I ordered the crew to bale out and we all managed to get out of the drivers bale out door, which was on the side away from the enemy. We were then in view of the Germans, so I ordered a trench to be dug under the tank, as this seemed the best and safest way to defend ourselves. After the trench was dug, as you may guess, we got our petrol stove out and made some tea! About two hundred yards to our right was a farmhouse, it was on fire, and as we sat drinking our tea watching it, the door opened and a German Officer and another soldier came out waving a white flag on a stick, so I cautiously waved them forward. The officer spoke good English and he said they wished to surrender, so I said, "Very good, sit down and have some tea". However he then asked if we were British, American or Canadian, and I proudly told him that we were English.

His answer surprised us, as he said, "If you are English then I wish to surrender my company to you." So I asked him what would have been his reply if I had said we were American, and his answer was that German soldiers thought it an insult to surrender to an American, as they did not consider them to be good soldiers. I then ordered him to send his soldier back to the farmhouse then return with his company. I also said that if the soldier did not return or anything went wrong, I would shoot him. The soldier did return with about fifty others, they all came out of the blazing farmhouse in single file, without arms and sat down in front of us. I apologised to the officer that I could not possibly make tea for such a large number of soldiers, and we had a laugh about this. While all this was taking place, the other four members of my crew were covering the company with small arms. I struggled back into the tank through the drivers bale out door, and with difficulty climbed into the turret. In order to radio all this information to HQ I was ordered to escort the prisoners with another member of my crew, to Infantry HQ about a mile back, and hand them over. I explained to the German officer that we would walk in single file, he would be first and I would walk behind him. This was so that if any funny business started behind I would shoot him. The prisoners were behind me and were covered from the rear by my crew member. I had been given a map reference of the HQ, and as we walked in single file I had an eerie feeling that numerous members of the enemy were watching us in field glasses.

We found the Infantry HQ it was a group of farm buildings surrounded by a wall about ten feet high. We handed the Germans over then made for the entrance of the compound to make our way back to our tank. Just at that moment about five mortar bombs landed around us, and I felt something hit the right side of my right knee. It was not that painful, and when I looked down I saw it was a small piece of metal about the size and shape of a darning needle sticking out of my knee. Reaching down I pulled it out and threw it away, not realising the trouble this would cause me later.

We then left the compound to make our way back to Apollo. After about a quarter of a mile, we walked into a field in which one of our tanks was burning fiercely when we heard a shout coming from the direction of the burning tank. After hearing the shout for a second time, we went in that direction, and about twenty feet from the tank in a deep furrow we found Arthur Egerton another one of my friends. He came from Hollinwood, near Manchester. He could not move, and when I asked what had happened, he replied that when the tank was hit he had baled out of the operator flaps onto the right hand track and then jumped. The snatch plug had not worked, and the cord had pulled him up short making him land on the track on his back before he had rolled on to the ground. We found out later that he had broken his back, though he said he had no pain. The Germans must have seen us then for a dozen or so small mortar bombs started to fall around us. I explained to Arthur that we had better go, but made him a promise that I would come back when it was dark. We made it back to Apollo, and we were by then extremely hungry, so after making all the guns useless in case the Germans came back, we nipped over to the farmhouse, taking our sub-machine guns and our revolvers with us. We did find some food; we found some bread, potatoes and vegetables and also a live chicken.

We chopped the head off the chicken and put it in the pan with everything else. Providentially everything was burning except the kitchen, and we even found a tablecloth, which was ceremoniously put on the table. After boiling this wondrous stew for a time, we all sat around the table in a very civilised way and had dinner; we were only short of a bottle of wine. When dinner was over, and it was getting dark, we radioed back to HQ that two of us were going back to Arthur, and asked them to send an ambulance to the map reference I had already given. My driver and I then went on our way back to Arthur. We came to a ditch across a field and as I jumped across, I heard a noise below me, and on landing on the other side, I noticed a hole in the ditch, and out of this came three Germans, an officer, a soldier and a Red Cross man. The soldier put his guns on the ground and the officer gave me his Luger pistol and his binoculars. (These binoculars I managed to get home and my grandson Neil now has them). When I explained to them what we were doing, the Red Cross man interpreted this to the other two as he spoke some English. We explained that Arthur had back trouble and he said we would need a stretcher, then he went off saying he would find something. We told him where to find us and off he went. The four of us then made our way back to Arthur. We had not been with him more than five minutes when the Red Cross man arrived with a house door. We were very lucky to have him, as he explained how to roll Arthur onto a ground sheet and

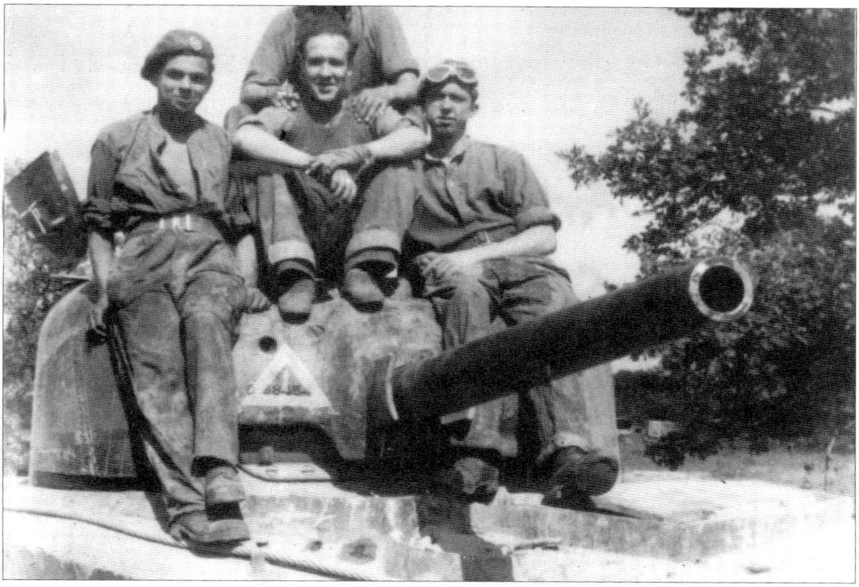

Col. Arthur Egerton (centre) A Squadron, 51st Royal Tank Regiment

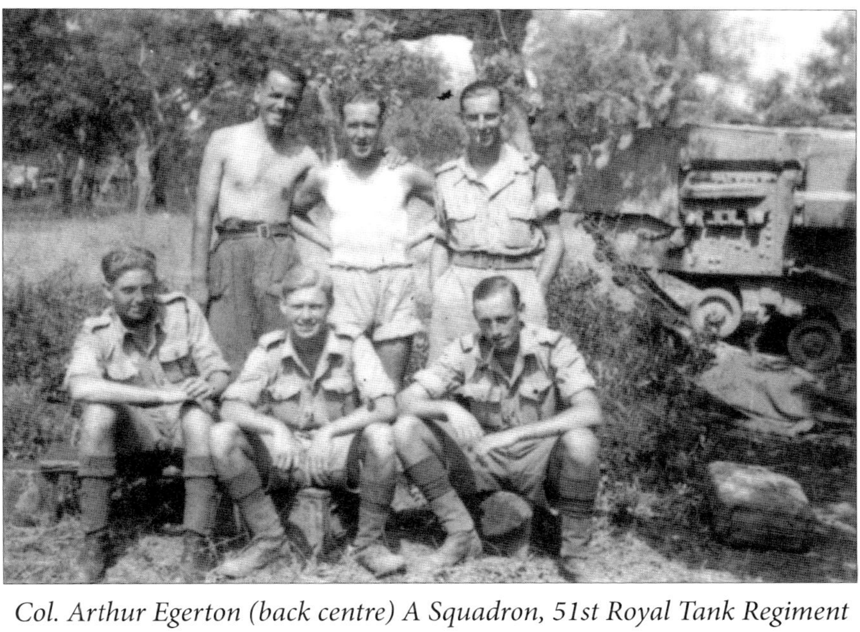

Col. Arthur Egerton (back centre) A Squadron, 51st Royal Tank Regiment

not to lift anyone with back trouble as this could aggravate it. Then all of us lifted the ground sheet onto the door, keeping his back straight all the time. The journey back was undertaken with great difficulty, and took us three hours. It was pitch black and we dare not show a light.

Arthur said he had no pain, because below his shoulders was numb. When we arrived at Apollo I got on the radio to see if they were coming, but it seems they had made three attempts with different ambulances, but with no success. They were now sending a Churchill tank up, as that was the only vehicle capable of getting to us. About an hour and a half later, the crew cursing and swearing, as like us they were unable to use lights and they had a terrible job trying to find us. When they eventually found us, they helped us to lift the door with Arthur tied on to it, onto the top of the drivers' and co-drivers' positions. The co-driver stayed on top, and with the three Germans would hold the door and Arthur in place. Before moving off, I climbed up to see if he was all right. He asked me to write to his wife to explain that as soon as he was able he would write to her. This I did promise him, and away they went, vanishing into the dark. Unfortunately on the way back, he died. I did write to his wife about a week later, she answered asking me to call at her house when I eventually went home, and I replied that I would.

* * *

CHAPTER TEN

Hospitalisation, leave and marriage

It was after Rimini that the clicking in my right knee became more noticeable, and earlier I had cut the back of my left leg on some protruding wire, while slipping off the tank. The first aid man had put some stitches in for me but I had since opened it again and it was festering a little, so I thought it was time to visit the Medical Officer. He dealt with the left leg, but he said that the right knee needed to be looked at by a specialist. So after getting together what little kit I possessed, I was loaded on a truck going to Ancona, about forty miles down the coast, where I reported to a military hospital. This hospital was originally one of Mussolini's army barracks. It was on the side of the main road going north/south, it was made of concrete, no doors on the wards, no paint on the walls, no windows, and the traffic on the road outside was all military and never stopped day or night.

The day after I arrived I had to have a full medical as well as having my knee checked. The doctor explained that the splinter of shrapnel that had stuck in my knee had by an unlucky chance, stuck between the knee joint and the cartilage had started to split. As time went on it would split more and more, and so he would take the cartilage out. A couple of days later I had to strip and lie on my side on a marble slab put my arms behind my knees and pull up to open my vertebrae. They then injected into my spine so that a little while after I became numb from the waist down. I was allowed to watch the operation from a large mirror on the ceiling, and I was very apprehensive when I found that they were using tools more fitting for a garage than an operating theatre. They were using crowbars, and saws and it looked like a joiners shop. When it was all over, I was given morphine and taken back to my bed. A few hours later feeling started to come back, in my body and my legs, but not to my penis, so every now and then I put my hand under the sheet to make sure it was still there. About twelve hours later it came back to life, to my undying relief. I think this frightened me more than the German Tiger tanks had!

For soldiers in this hospital, life was very embarrassing. Those from the RAF and from other units had their pyjamas, but the soldiers from the front had nothing, and when the time came for taking exercise they had to walk up and down without a stitch on in front of the young nurses, which was very embarrassing. When we asked for pyjamas we were told that none were available. While I was in hospital, the RAF transport people started to bring in wounded Yugoslavs, one planeload each night. There were men and women, and they were put into any bed that was available, which made things even worse, as they also had nothing to wear. Any patients not bedridden had to do anything that was needed, like getting bedpans and helping them feeding, cleaning the wards and washing up the feeding utensils, and also helping to wash the other patients. It was all quite a mess and not very pleasant, which did not help with recuperation.

The Yugoslavs seemed to us at that time to be not very nice people, and very untrustworthy; all cupboards had to be locked, and at night we British had to sleep with everything we possessed under our pillows, even our boots, pens and pencils and letters, as they would steal anything and everything,this was probably because of the terrible conditions they had been living in.

When the Yugoslavs were no longer bedridden patients, they were kitted out with British Army uniforms, as they had no clothes, but they wore a red star on their headgear. When eventually they were allowed out in the afternoons, we would hear reports of robberies from shops and houses. They would remove their headgear with the red star on and put them into their coat pockets, they would then look like British soldiers.

The time came when eventually I was told that I was being sent to a convalescent camp in the south of Italy, because everything had been done that was necessary and it was only time now for my knee to heal. When the day of my move from hospital came, two others and myself were ordered to have an FFI check. (Free From Infection). The FFI check was carried out on all British personnel moving from one unit to another. The other two soldiers moving on the same day and myself dutifully lined up outside the Medical Officers room. As my name began with A, as usual I was first on the list.

It was normal procedure to go into the room with only trousers on, stand in front of the doctor, your hands would be inspected, then the mouth and throat, then you would be ordered to "Drop them". You immediately dropped your trousers, and would then be checked for venereal disease. When my name was called, I opened the door and walked in wearing only my trousers. I then received a shock, as there before me was a lady doctor, and a nurse at her side. They must have been recent arrivals from Britain, as they were both very white with no sign of a tan. My hands and mouth were inspected, then she said, "Drop them", which I did. She leaned forward with a pencil in her hand, and to my great embarrassment proceeded to lift my penis with it. To my even greater embarrassment the nurse who was only about twenty years of age, burst out laughing. I went red in the face, and the doctor pointed to the door and told the nurse to get out, promising to see her later. She went out still choking with laughter, and the doctor apologised to me as I pulled up my trousers. I grabbed my FFI certificate and beat a hasty retreat.

I was issued with a new uniform, and though it did not fit at least it was clean, and I also got soap and razor blades etc., which were gratefully received. The two others and myself very gingerly boarded a truck, and were driven to the docks in Ancona, where we boarded a hospital ship bound for Bari in the south of Italy. The journey south was uneventful, and on arrival at Bari after waiting for some hours, I was taken by truck to the small town of Trani, where the convalescent camp was about two miles behind the town. I found to my dismay that this was also an ex Mussolini army barracks, identical to the hospital in Ancona. This one had a twelve feet high wall all around it. Unlike the convalescent camps shown on films this one was staffed by physical training experts. I had been hoping to see a staff of lovely British nurses with cups of tea served with nice soft hands!

However, all I received was a physical training sergeant snarling at me, "You're in barrack room 18, bed number fourteen." I signed in, and then went searching for my bed. Half an hour later I found it, it was in a room with all the beds in tiers of three bunks.

My bed was the middle one, which was about four feet up from the floor. A chap named Harry was in the bottom bunk, he came from the Durham Light Infantry and was from near Ipswich. We got on very well together, and he had been there a few weeks. I found he was known by the name of Heinz, this was because he had trodden on a shoe mine, which had caused fifty-seven gashes to his legs, body and face. He had very nearly died but now he was at the camp to get fit again and then to rejoin his regiment. A shoe mine is a German anti-personnel mine made only of wood and glass, which consequently could not be detected. Harry surprised me by telling me that any penicillin was reserved only for the RAF, the army was not allowed any. It meant that if an RAF man cut his finger peeling potatoes he could have penicillin, but Harry with fifty-seven gashes could not have any. It made me wonder how many army personnel could have been saved if they had been allowed just a little penicillin.

We all had to take turns at barrack room duties, like washing the floor every day then pouring paraffin on and spreading it in every nook and cranny to kill all the bugs. This was done daily and we were allowed half a gallon of paraffin a week. All patients (yes we were called patients!) were allowed out for a half-day each week and we were allowed the princely sum of five shillings to spend. So every Thursday afternoon Harry and I would walk the two miles into town to our favourite café, where we would have two lots of coffee and cognac, then walk back again. Not a very exciting life. One day an American came in and we got talking. He asked why we had no medals when we had been in the forces so long and had fought in Africa, Italy and Sicily. He told us that he had been in the forces for one and a half years and had three full rows of medals. He wanted to buy a round of drinks, but we had to refuse as we had no more money and could not reciprocate. He said that we were too proud and that pride was our downfall. He drew a big roll of notes from his pocket and said that if one of us would just lower our pride and say, "Can I have that?" he would give it to us. He added that we must not think it would leave him broke as he was in charge of three P.X.s (the equivalent of our Naafi) on three American aerodromes, and he could make over a thousand dollars a day without risk. That made us even more stubborn. However it was all very interesting to us.

We were in Trani one day when the funeral of a priest came along the road followed by a party of orphan boys with monks in charge of them. It was an inch deep in snow, and all that the boys were wearing was thin cotton shirts and shorts, and they were all bare footed, while the monks had on thick brown habits and climbing boots. One little boy dropped his candle in the snow, he must have been so cold that his hands were numb, but one of the monks strolled up to him and punched him in the face knocking him down into the snow. The poor little boy was then wet making him even colder. We were distressed at the rough treatment they got and how little mercy was shown to them.

Harry was a wonderful person, he had volunteered to fight for his country, had been severely wounded, He was 22 years of age, had fought in Tunisia and Italy and was getting fit to fight again for his people and country, I considered him to be a fine person. The day came when he was pronounced fit and was sent on his way back to his regiment, the Durham Light Infantry.

A few days later I was called in to see the Commanding Officer, and he explained that the papers concerning me had just arrived, and because my left eye was not good, I had been slightly down graded, and therefore I would not be returning to my regiment. I was to be sent to a re-allocation unit in Reitti. However the next day I was called in again, and I was really shocked when he asked me if I would be interested in two weeks home leave. Obviously I jumped at the chance, as I was not really entitled to any leave, as this was not allowed until after four years service abroad. About a week later I was taken to an RAF field where with a few others I was taken aboard a Lancaster Bomber bound for Norwich. There were no seats so we all sat on the floor. All the others were Infantry men who had been abroad for at least four years, and had been up and down the North African desert a couple of times. I felt a little embarrassed, and an impostor, not having served as long as them abroad. The trip was very boring, and there were one or two arguments between the crew and the Infantry lads, who felt they were very hard done by compared with the rations given to the RAF personnel.

We landed in Norwich and were given railway warrants, and ration cards for two weeks. Then we were given the time and date of our return, and also threatened with what would happen to us if we were late on returning. We were all taken to Norwich railway station and boarded the train for London. All trains from Norwich went to London, and on our way we were all surprised at how everything looked so green after being in the Middle East for so long, and also that all the school children spoke English! It sounds so ridiculous but it really did hit us like that. We were lucky not to have a hold up, and quickly arrived in London. In wartime it was so normal to have a hold up, some even lasting a whole day.

On arrival in London I went immediately to the enquiries office and joined the queue. My turn came about an hour later, and I enquired about the time for a train to Manchester. I was horrified when the answer was "In fifteen hours time". I must have had such a murderous look on my face because he said, "I am sorry but there is nothing before that". It was then that a girl behind me in the queue tapped me on the shoulder and asked me what the man had said as she was also going to Manchester. We commiserated with each other then went to the café and had a cup of tea. She asked me where I would be able to sleep and I told her somewhere in the station on the floor as I had two blankets with me. She said that she had already booked a room in the hotel opposite the station and would I like to join her there, and I did.

The next day we travelled to Manchester, it was pleasant to have company and it was a reasonably normal journey.

On arrival I hoisted my belongings out, which consisted of my bag, two army blankets, a sub machine gun with ammunition and a revolver with ammunition. Then I put my best foot forward to walk to Stevenson's Square to catch a number 24 bus to Royton. Carrying that load made me sweat, and not thinking I loosened the buttons on my uniform.

Two minutes later two Military Police Red Caps stepped in front of me with book and pen at the ready to book me. I noticed as they looked at my shoulders where I had the maple leaf awarded to us, that they were Canadians and they said, "We have been told to look out for your mob". He put his book and pencil away and

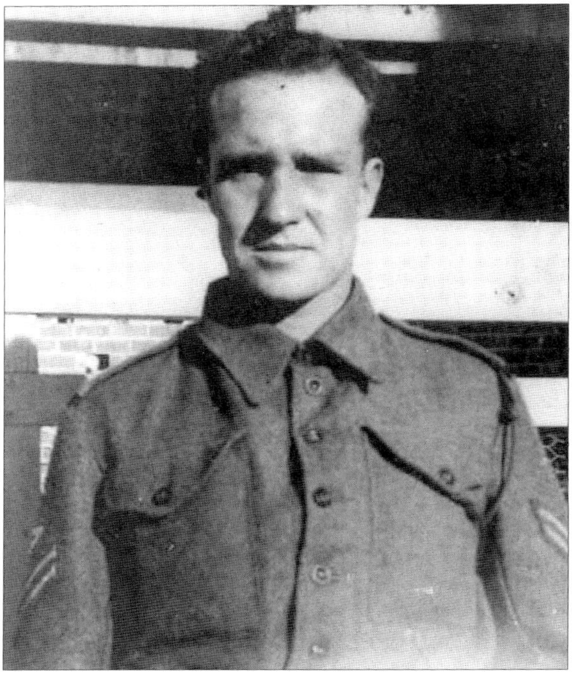

Cpl Arthur Egerton

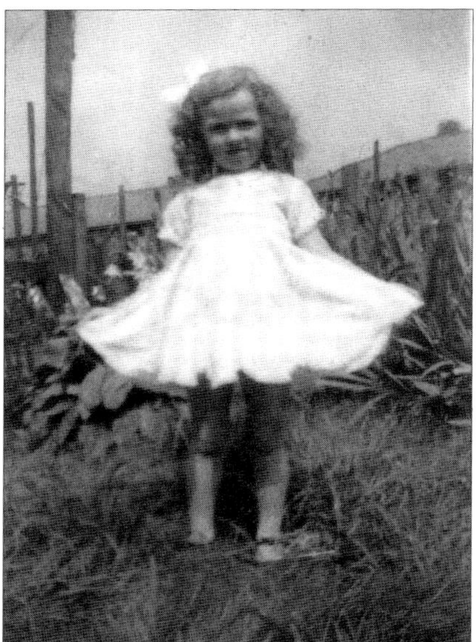

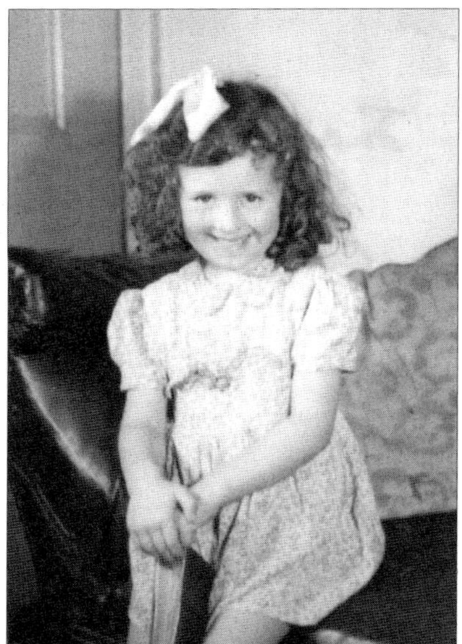

Visiting Judith, aged 3, when on leave in 1945

insisted that they carry everything except my arms to the bus about a quarter of a mile away, and even insisted that they would carry them on the bus for me. I thanked them profusely and they shook hands with me as if I was their long lost brother.

The bus had only been going for about five minutes when I felt a tap on my shoulder again and on looking round saw a young lady who asked, "Are you Frank Ashworth?" I did not recognise her but she assured she had met me on one of my previous leaves, before going to Africa. We chatted about old times and she asked me to call on her the next day, but said that if the books in her window were standing up I must walk past, but if they were laying down I was to walk into the house through the unlocked door. I felt this was a bit suspicious, like something from a spy novel! She left the bus about a mile before I did.

Walking from the bus to home, I felt very conspicuous and embarrassed; I must have looked like an overloaded Christmas tree.

During my absence the family had moved to a semi-detached council house near the park in Royton. It was a great relief to get inside the house, where Mam and Dad and Joseph were waiting. I had informed them I was coming, but could not say when. Mam seemed so happy and was actually surprised that I had survived; I think her mind had been back in 1914 when her then fiancé George Baron had gone to war and never came back. A bottle of beer was put in front of me, these being scarce then, and within half an hour the biggest dinner I had seen for a long time was put in front of me, in spite of the rationing, and I am sure she thought I had not eaten for years, and indeed it did feel like that.

As promised to Arthur Egerton before he died, this being the first opportunity I had, I called to see his wife, but on knocking at the door a lady came out and I asked if she was Arthur's wife. She said no but please come in and she went on to explain that Arthur's wife had died about a month after Arthur and this lady was his wife's sister and had inherited the house and adopted the child who it is doubtful he had ever seen. I wished her well and left, never knowing that there would be another meeting with the child sixty years later.

The next day I went to Doreen's to see how everyone was going on. She lived only about five miles from me, and during the day we decided to get married on the following Saturday. We caught a bus to Manchester in order to get a special licence, which we delivered to the vicar of St Chad's Church, New Moston. Doreen's parents would arrange a reception at their house. I found a friend of mine, Tommy Malloney who would be my best man. On my wedding day I caught the bus to St. Chad's Church, I couldn't find the vicar, but I eventually found him gardening, it seems he had forgotten all about the wedding! He dashed to the church still in his muddy boots, just in time for the Bentley family and Doreen to arrive. The marriage took place, and then we all went to the Bentley house for the reception. Someone had managed to acquire a small barrel of beer, which obviously came in handy. Being wartime, there was no chance of having a honeymoon so we stayed at the Bentley house and next day we went to register the marriage.

It soon became the day I had to return to Norwich, and Doreen came to the station to see me off.

On the way down to London, I did wonder if I had done the right thing. I changed trains in London and eventually arrived in Norwich. The weather was atrocious and there was no chance of any planes taking off. There were about fifty of us waiting for transport, everyone being from a fighting regiment, and we were all allocated a Sunday School Hall for accommodation for the night. During the evening in parties of two or three we all went into Norwich, returning to the School Hall within a couple of hours.

We all had the same tale to tell, no publican would serve us with a drink unless we paid double for it as the Americans were.

We could not afford these prices on our pay, and it irked us that all of us had been in the front line fighting for longer than any of the Americans had even been in the war.

I would also say that nine out of ten of these Americans were only ground staff, and had never been out of England or seen an angry face. It made us ashamed of these greedy publicans who turned up their noses at the men who were fighting for their freedom.

A few days later we were still waiting for transport, so a few of us went out again, when coming towards us we saw an American with an English girl, and for some unknown reason he suddenly hit her. We all saw red, as having worked near some Americans in Italy and Sicily, we found that next to the Italians they were some of the biggest rogues going and to see one hit a girl like that riled us.

One of our crowd went over and beat up the American, then some more Americans arrived and we all joined in the fighting. Soon a crowd of over eighty were battling it out, when whistles sounded and about fifty British Military Police arrived on the scene, also the same number of American Military Police arrived all armed with sub-machine guns, and managed eventually to separate us out. The British Military Police escorted us back to the Sunday School Hall, but we were not charged. The weather continued to be terrible, but two days later we continued our journey back to Italy by train instead of by air as originally intended.

We went via London to Dover, where we boarded a ship to Calais, on which only service personnel were allowed on board. A few days later together with a hundred or so infantrymen, we entrained for Italy. The journey proved uneventful, we went through Paris during the night and through to Switzerland the next day. Then we went through the Simplon Tunnel and arrived on the other side at a town called Domodosala, the first town in Italy. We carried on South for a few more hours and eventually arrived at a town and detrained, but I cannot remember the name of the town. Shortly after I found myself in Ruetti and this was a period of time of utter boredom.

* * *

CHAPTER ELEVEN

Back to Italy and demobilisation

As soon as I arrived back in Italy I had to cancel my allowance to my mother and sign it over to Doreen, and I do not think Mam would have been very happy about that.

Not long after this we found out that the war in Europe was over, though nobody had thought to tell us! There were no celebrations, not even a bottle of beer was to be had.

Soon after this about fifty of us, all of the Royal Tank Regiment, were made into a tank delivery squadron in order to move up into Austria to establish a depot at a small town called Udendorf. This was about twenty miles from Klagenfurt. We set of in convoy taking with us eight tanks of various sizes and some armoured cars. The journey was about four hundred miles, but we broke it in Bologna, and late on the second day we crossed the frontier post from Italy into Austria.

We stopped about two hundred yards from the border and out of a little wooden hut on the hill came a little boy and girl of about eight years of age. They stopped about thirty yards away, and I spoke to them saying "Good Day" to them in German. The little boy clicked his heels together and bowed his head, the little girl curtsied, and they returned the compliment, saying "Good Day". It forcibly hit me that all the way up Italy we had never known any politeness from anyone, be it adult or child, and most were begging and stealing, and here were two lovely children who were supposed to be our enemies.

We arrived at our destination later in the day; this was a number of small wooden huts close to a graveyard in Udendorf. Unfortunately the supposedly slave labour consisting of Hungarians were still there. The next day soldiers arrived with rifles to force them out of the huts onto a train, which would take them back to Hungary. However, they did not want to go home, as they said that during their stay in Austria they had been very happy and made friends with the Austrians, and did not want to return to the poverty of their own country, but the authorities insisted that they return to Hungary.

We then took over the camp, and I remember looking through the little window of the hut I lived in, to see a large square gravestone with the name Wilhelm Kaiser carved on it.

Life was extremely hard for the Austrians, there was very little food and everyone even the babies were issued hard tack biscuits. The British took over the area from the Russians; most of them had been Mongolian Russians. When we first arrived the women and girls looked quite ugly, as they had all shaved off their hair, but we soon found out why. Every Saturday night by order of the Russians every female over twelve had to report to the Guasthouse, then every officer would take their pick, after which the men would then have their pick. The only way the women could retaliate was to cut off their hair, wear old and dirty clothes and be dirty and smelly.

All their good clothing had been buried in the fields and gardens. When we arrived, there was a flurry of digging in the gardens to recover their clothing, furniture and valuables. They were so happy to be rid of the Russians.

Gratz was also taken over by the British from the Russians, and during this take over, a Salvation Army detachment brought up a small van in order to issue tea and buns to the troops. Then one day the van was stolen, and an Austrian had seen two Russian soldiers take it. The Salvation Army reported this to the Russian Commandant and two days later he sent for them and told them that their van had been recovered and the culprits punished. The van was round the back of the building and upon opening it the Salvation Army people found the two Russians dead inside the van. They were appalled at this drastic punishment.

I remember that it was at about this time that an order of the day came to all units in Europe. It stated that all British Units in Italy or France had to be armed on leaving their Regimental quarters, though all units in Germany and Austria need not carry arms away from Regimental areas. It seemed very strange that in enemy countries we need not be armed, but in so called friendly countries we had to carry arms as we may be in danger.

A couple of weeks after arriving in Udendorf, I had just returned to my little hut after enjoying a good dinner in the cook house, bringing back two large cheese sandwiches for later. I put the sandwiches in a box. Then I heard some children crying and looking out of the window I saw a little boy and girl of about four or five years of age, sitting on a gravestone, and when I asked them why they were crying, they answered that they were hungry and their stomachs hurt. I could do nothing other than hand over my two cheese sandwiches, but they would not accept them. Upon asking why this was, they said that their father had told them they must not accept anything they had not worked for. So, putting on a stern look, I said they must come and work for me, and I gave them each a boot to clean, and when they had finished I said they were not clean enough and they must clean them again, which they did. I then presented the two cheese sandwiches and told them to eat. The boy then pointed to a piece of paper on the bed and asked if he could have it to wrap the sandwiches in, because their mother and father and other sisters were also hungry, and they could all share the sandwiches. I was overwhelmed by these two youngsters being so considerate of their family, so I again put on a stern face and said that they must come every day, as I had lots of work for them to do.

So every day they turned up and I found it very difficult to find enough jobs for them to do, but every day I managed to scrounge something from the cookhouse for them. The strange thing is that their names were Hansel and Grettel.

When I found out that it was near to Hansel's Birthday I tried to find him a present, but there was nothing in any of the shops. However, I found a farmer who was willing to sell me a piglet, and I gave this to Hansel telling him that every day I would give him the cookhouse swill to take home.

When the time came for me to leave Udendorf to go home, I was invited to their little wooden house on the hillside and they all thanked me for what I had done for them, and then asked if I would choose anything I saw in the house to take for a thank you present. I pretended to look around, but I thought I could not take anything from them, and then I saw a little brooch, which had two children on it like Hansel and Grettel, so I asked for the brooch saying that it would remind me of the children. I still have that brooch to this day.

Christmas was a very quiet time, especially for the Austrians with the shortage of food. However the marvellous views all around were certainly like Christmas card views, with all the mountains and snow, and the clear skies with millions of stars. My friend and I decided to go for a walk on New Year's Eve before turning into bed, and we were passing a typical Austrian house when two young ladies came out and said their father had asked them to invite us in to join the family party. We were introduced to everyone from the grandmother down to the children, and were invited to join them to share their drinks and food. One of them started to play the piano accordion and the singing and dancing started. We thoroughly enjoyed ourselves on a night that we had expected to be a bit lonely, and on the stroke of midnight everyone shook hands and wished each other far happier times ahead. When we took our leave, they all streamed out into the street to see us off, shouting their farewells and wishes for our happiness, we were extremely touched and thought what lovely people they were.

A few months later we decided to put on a dance, and managed to acquire six musicians from the band of the l6/5th Lancers who were stationed about twenty-five miles away. We arranged sandwiches and cakes made in the cookhouse, and somehow we found some beer. Many of the young ladies from the village came, and all had a wonderful evening, except one young lady through no fault of her own who actually fell into a cesspit! She was quickly rescued and taken off by some of the young ladies to be cleaned up.

For some reason that I cannot remember now I somehow got into a fight with the Colonel's Batman of the l6/5th Lancers, we were quickly separated, and the batman was kicked out. That was my last serious fight, as since then I have never wanted to again.

One young lady, I think was called Anna, asked me to her house to meet her family. A few days later I called as asked, and found that her family was quite an important one in the district. During the conversation, I innocently stated that I had trodden on Anna's foot while we were dancing. They all went red and it was explained to me that Foot in their language was a very rude word, and that I should have said Foos, the German Word for foot.

We very often had to deliver vehicles to other parts of Austria, but most of the time we were taking and delivering to Regiments in Italy. After delivering we would then pick up other vehicles from Udini and Bologna to take back to Austria. Some of these journeys through the Southern Alps in winter were extremely hard and dangerous because of the biting cold, and ice. There were no heating systems or windscreens in armoured vehicles, so we wore everything we possessed, even wrapping tarpaulin round our shoulders arms and head, cutting eye holes in them. On one of these trips I bought a lightweight raincoat and a ladies wristwatch for Doreen. To make sure this watch got safely to her, I opened a tube of toothpaste, squeezed out the paste, then threaded the wristwatch into it, then sealed it. The reason this was necessary was the amount of pilfering taking place in both the army and civilian post offices, but it did reach its destination safely.

During my time in Austria, the British Government issued a circular stating that should any serving personnel wish to continue further education on demobilisation, this could be arranged. The education would be free and a weekly allowance, including marriage allowances etc. would be available. I applied for this, but the reply from the government was that only those with certificates of education from before the war would be eligible. So once again I was frustrated. That was my last chance, so as the saying goes, I just had to soldier on. Looking back on that, I now realise that the powers that be at that time were making sure that the people who had money enough for education pre-war were the ones who would benefit for refresher courses and advanced courses after the war.

I got friendly with one or two of the villagers, and they were pleased when I complimented them on the lovely open-air swimming pool they had there. They told me that pre-war, Adolph Hitler had ordered that every town and village must have a swimming pool mainly for health and recreation purposes. But when the pools froze in winter to a depth of about four feet, they provided a lovely skating rink enjoyed by all ages. Then when spring arrived the villagers would cut the ice into blocks, and these would be distributed to each house to put down in the cellar, which then provided cold storage for meats etc. until the next winter. I thought this was a great idea, as this was before anyone had a refrigerator, as we know it to day.

As time went on the Russians were gradually pushed out of Austria and more food was shipped in, so in every sense things were improving for everyone.

A couple of times I went horse riding, and being a complete novice did not feel very confident. The second time we went, we had just come out of the forest and were near to a railway track when a train came by hooting as it went. The horse bolted with me hanging on for dear life. I eventually fell off but managed to hang onto the horse and get him under control again. However, I would not get back on and walked him all the way home. There ended my horse riding days, as I never got on one again.

We heard that demobilisation was starting, and this set me thinking very deeply, as I had been in the army from 17 years of age, and had been living with men, fought against and with men, had been frightened many times, and had been very lucky several times, with the kind of luck that is even more supreme than winning the lottery, as I had come out alive when all the odds had been against it. I had for a period of a few years lost many good friends who had been the cream of manhood and the fittest of the country. Men who deserved the greatest of praise, which nowadays is only given to the glamorous units, and not to the men who did it away from the headlines and cameras, and who died without recognition. My greatest loss was David Owen, or to be correct Captain David Owen, who was my best-loved friend and a man amongst men. The man who was killed only about ten seconds after saving my life, and I will openly admit I have shed many tears for him, and he was only 22 years of age when he died. He was worth at least two Victoria Crosses, with the actions I saw him perform, but as these actions were not witnessed by a commanding officer, they were not eligible.

In action periods, especially in Africa, we almost became like wild men. Anything we owned was fastened on the outside of the tank, and was destroyed during action. As many of the essential supplies were being pilfered on the way from the suppliers to ourselves in the front line, we were lacking in things such as soap, toothpaste and towels. Also we never had any mugs or plates, no change of underwear or top clothes, no creams for rashes, nor razor blades or toilet paper. Eventually we became very uncivilised! However, for some unknown reason we became more considerate towards each other. In most cases we would go to extremes to help others in the squadron. These conditions certainly bonded us together, sometimes even to risking our lives. I think it is this bonding that civilians and non-combatant service personnel cannot understand. Even when explained they find it impossible to comprehend. Also people can never understand why men of the line can never forget. Many people consider them boring and dull, they just do not want to know. I think they cannot possibly imagine what life is like when the only options are life or death. It is such a tension that one cannot be rid of it, no matter how many years pass.

I thought very deeply about civilian life and all the petty things associated with it, and my conclusion was that I only wanted to be a tramp, and not have to bother with all the formalities of civilisation. This was at the time my only ambition. It sounds so strange but quite honestly this was all I wanted to do, to go where I wanted at any time and do what I wanted when I wanted, to have no responsibilities except finding something to eat. I was torn between my responsibilities of being a married man and my feelings at the time of wanting to opt out. Eventually of course I realised that it was the cowardly way out, and accepted that I must return to a conventional way of life after being demobilised when the time came. Everything carried on as normal, except that sometimes life did not feel normal at all. It often felt more of a threat. The last seven years had been my formative years, I had been moulded into a tank soldier and I hardly knew anything else. To be truthful I was frightened and very nervous. I know that fear was normal for men of the line, I had known extreme fear during times in action, it seemed to ease off when I was commanding, but I think that was because I tried not to show it in front of men in my care. But this was a different fear, in that it was fear of the unknown, not knowing the prices of commodities, having to compete for jobs, and having to say the right things. It was now that I realised I had lived an uncivilised life for so long that the thought of a normal life worried me.

In June 1946 when my papers arrived ordering me to report to the Austrian town of Klagenfurt, I and two others said our goodbyes to our friends, ordered a fifteen hundred weight truck, and were taken to a military establishment in Klagenfurt, where we joined about five hundred others. We were told that we would only be allowed in England, with issued articles only. Anything we had acquired had to be thrown into a heap in the centre of the parade ground. Of course previous to that we had handed in our weapons such as revolvers and sub machine guns etc. When everyone had finished throwing their prized possessions on the heap, petrol was poured on and everything was set on fire, we almost cried. After that we were issued with a packet of sandwiches and told to fill our water bottles, then we were marched two hundred yards to the railway station, where we embarked on a train which was to take us to Dover. It was a dreary journey with only forces personnel on board; most of the journey was during the night, and we arrived at Calais to be embarked on a cross channel ferry to Dover.

Coaches were waiting for us on the quayside and these took us to a depot at Woking. A hot meal was served to us before we went to bed, and for this we were immensely grateful for we were all exhausted. The next day was the big day, we were all processed through and then finished up at Woking railway station dressed in civilian suits, with shirts and ties and light shoes, carrying our uniforms in a bag, and with railway warrants to take us to our homes. We were also informed that we would be on the reserves list for the rest of our lives.

So that was the end of my war, and my return to civilian life.

I thought I would like to do nothing but be a tramp and go wherever I wanted when I wanted with no resposibilities or ties. These days I would have been diagnosed as having PTSD, but in my day you just had to get on with it, and so I went back to civilisation and my responsibilities.

* * *

CHAPTER TWELVE

A move to Jersey and a new life

On my way home from demobilisation in Woking, the full impact of my change of lifestyle hit me. I was going home to a new wife, of whom I realised I knew very little. I had only been with her on a few days before going abroad, when on my rare leaves, and also the week when we married. I was going to live with my wife's parents of whom I knew even less. I had to claim my job back and work with strange men who would resent me as a threat to their jobs. Especially now that lots of wartime jobs had finished, and those who had been on war work had grabbed all the best jobs. It was frightening.

I tried to compare the life ahead to the life I was leaving behind. For hours on the journey home my mind went back to my regiment and our participation in the war, from Libya to Tunisia, Algeria, Italy and Austria. The many men who were killed, and the men wounded in body or mind. I was told that my regiment from landing in Africa to the end of the European war had 450% casualties. From the middle of 1942 to 1945 we had hundreds of days in action in the front line, mainly during the spring, summer and autumn months, as in the winter months we mainly came to a standstill because of the atrocious weather conditions. The ground was then impossible for us to move over. Even then we still had to be on full alert, in case any counter attacks came through. During these times we still lived out in the open without even tents, but I remember that not one of us ever caught a cold. It was amazing.

I was most hurt having to leave behind so many of my friends, who would never return as I have. Even now I wonder why I have been allowed the many extra years to live. Why? Every one of those men killed was A1 fitness, what a loss to Britain. However, I feel very privileged to have lived and worked with these men of quality, courage and resolution. Some of them were men amongst men. I am very proud to have served with them. My dear friend Captain David Owen was one of these, a true hero to whom I owe my life, and when he was killed he was only 22 years-old.

There are hundreds of stories I could tell, but these days I find most people are not interested, or get bored by war stories. I only included the few wartime stories earlier, because they are mainly about friends from around my hometown of Royton, Lancashire.

I could not imagine what my life ahead would be, I could only hope. My remuneration from the Country for the seven years of service, three years of which was in the front line, was a measly £42. With this I was expected to house and clothe myself and make provision for the future for my family and myself.

So it was with deep misgivings that I contemplated my future on that journey home from Woking to Manchester.

After getting back to work and to domestic life, I was overjoyed when in 1947 Doreen gave birth to my daughter Brenda.

I changed my job from panel beating as it was a strenuous and dirty job, and went into transport.

My daugthter Brenda eventually married and moved to Jersey and in 1979 Doreen passed away, and as I was depressed I decided to take early retirement.

My friend from army days, Norman Bentley who was living in Jersey with his second wife Maureen, also passed away that year leaving Maureen to run a large guest house on her own. When Maureen heard that I had retired she asked if I would come to Jersey and help run the guest house. I gladly did this and had another change of career.

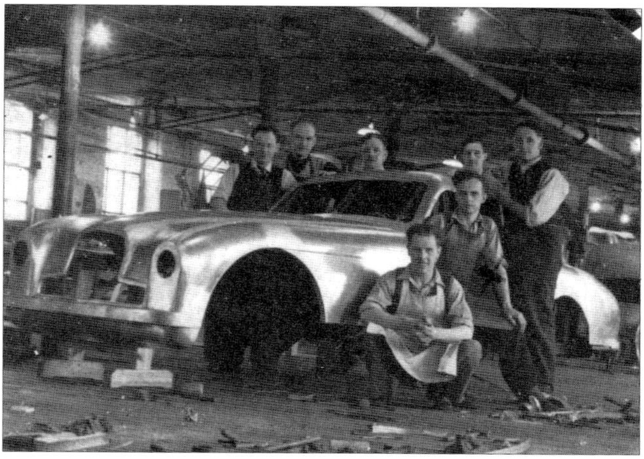

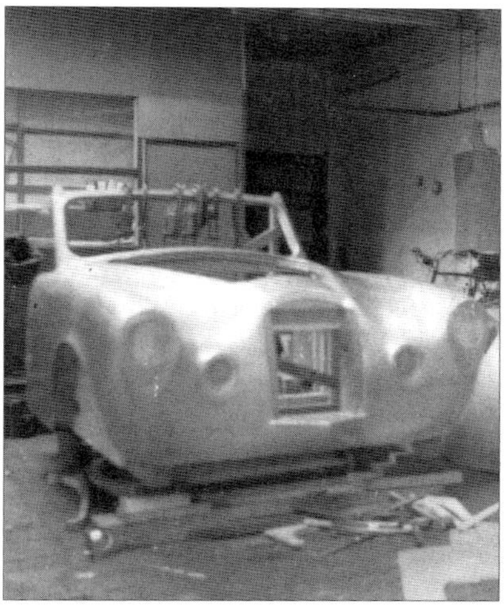

Panel beating
Aston Martins

After two years we got on so well and found love again and decided we had a future together so we married in 1982.

We then started to do some travelling which we had not had a chance to do before, and had decided to try and visit some of the war graves in the places where I had served. We contacted a company who were specialising in these holidays and booked to go round Italy in the May, 2002. They wrote and said that they did not have enough people so were cancelling this trip. The following year they wrote and said they were doing the trip again but we had already booked another holiday so could not go.

The following year 2004 when some friends talked about going on a cruise which took a route round Italy we decided to do it. The ship cruised round to Ancona which was where I had been in the war, and a few miles north was the Gradarra war graves cemetery. We took a taxi to the cemetery and I found numerous graves of my old comrades including David Owen and Arthur Egerton, which I found very emotional, this was sixty years after he had died. As we looked at Arthur's grave, there was a sheet of plastic covering a paper with a poem on it and it read "To Dad from Judith." We realised that must be Arthur's daughter who I had seen at the age of three when I was on leave and went to see Arthur's wife as I had promised. Her sister had opened the door to me and when I explained who I was and that I had come to see Arthur's widow, she invited me in and explained that Arthur's wife had died a month after Arthur had died. She and her husband had inherited the house and they had adopted Judith.

Not wanting to upset her adopted mother, Judith had not asked too much about her father and mother, until she passed away. She then tried to get as much information about her father as she could, but found no-one who had known him. She found where his grave was in Gradarra Cemetery and on the sixtieth anniversary of his death her husband David took her to Italy to see his grave and had left the poem and some flowers there.

When we were there, on leaving the cemetery we looked in the visitor's book and saw that a Judith Heyes from Manchester had visited only five days before and guessed that this was Arthur's daughter.

On returning home I looked in the Jersey Library for the Manchester Directory but there were too many Heyes to ring them all and we had not made a note of her husband's name. I then rang the British Legion in Manchester to see if they could help to trace her, but they were unable to do so. I almost gave up, but then decided to try the Salvation Army and found an office in the

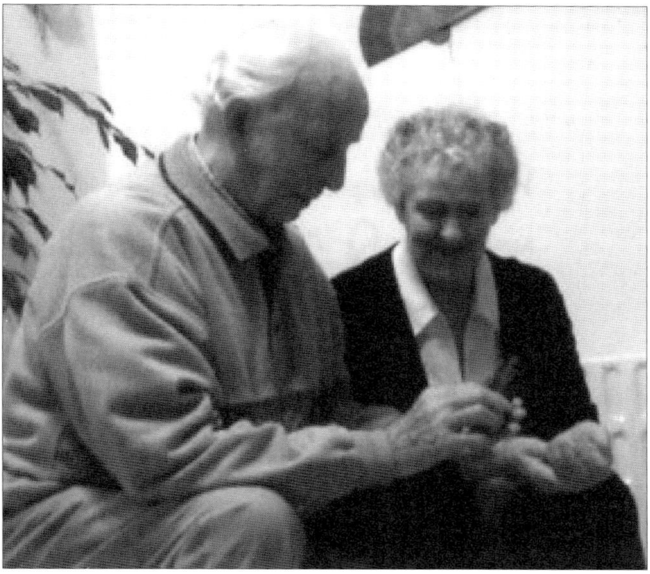

Frank explains the workings of the Churchill tank to Judith, 2005

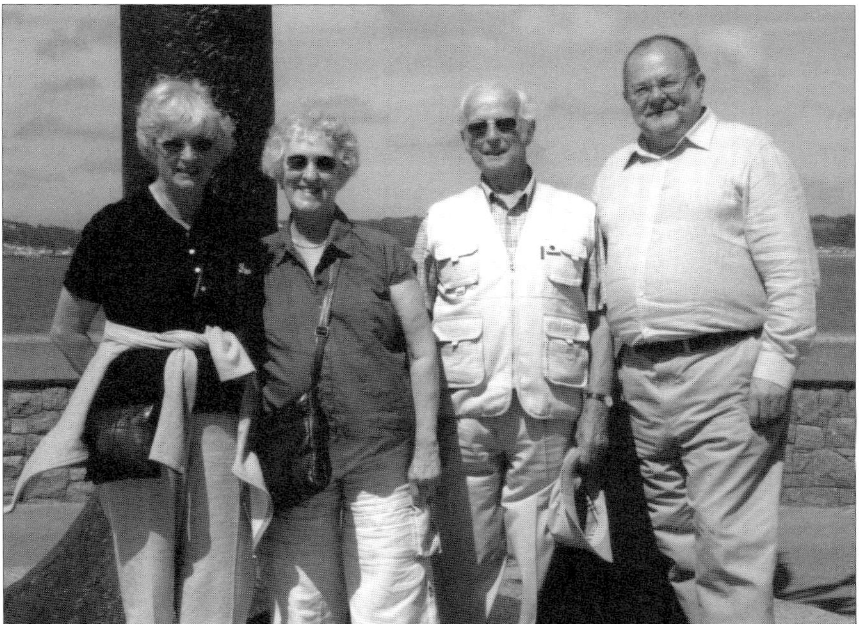

St Helier, July 2005: Maureen, Judith, Frank, David

Failsworth district which was where Arthur came from. On ringing the number an officer answered and when it was explained to him why I was trying to contact Judith he said he would do his very best but could not guarantee anything soon. However, on hearing the name of the person I was trying to locate he said that he actually knew a Judith Heyes, but it might not be the same person. He said he would make enquiries and let me know when he found anything. The next day there was a telephone call and it was a tearful lady on the line saying she was Judith Heyes and she would very much like to know more, but at that moment she was too emotional to talk and said she would ring back.

The next day she called and said that she and her husband David were coming to Jersey that weekend. Maureen and I arranged to meet them at the airport and there was an emotional greeting between Judith and myself. We went with them to their hotel and over afternoon tea Judith caught up with what had happened to her father. She said that all her life she had wanted to find someone who knew her father but without success. She had only gone to Italy after her adopted parents had both died as she did not want to upset them too much by searching the history of her father. David had taken her there on the anniversary of Arthur's death.

When we all met and she heard that I was the person who had actually found Arthur when he was wounded and managed to get him help and to hospital although he died after arriving there, it was so astounding to her to hear the full story and to know what had actually happened to him, and to find out what kind of a person he had been, she was over the moon and could not get over it.

It seems strange that Maureen and I had tried to get to Gradarra two years running without success, but had we gone on one of those trips we would not have been there five days after Judith and seen her name in the book, so would not have known anything about her.

The same guardian angel that had seen me through the war without harm must still have been looking out for me and for Judith.

We are still in touch with Judith and David and they are very considerate of me and appreciate what I did in finding Judith.

I feel content that something good came out of it all.

* * *

EPILOGUE

When Frank was 90 Brenda and Maureen had his medals mounted with the ribbons, which were still in the boxes sent from the War Office in 1947. They cajoled him into wearing them one Remembrance Sunday ceremony. He wore them twice.

He died in Jersey at the age of 97, knowing his Family were all there, but his heart was still in Royton.